African
American
Voices

The Life Cycle of Slavery

African American Voices

The Life Cycle of Slavery

Edited by
STEVEN MINTZ

BRANDYWINE PRESS • St. James, New York

ISBN 1-881089-11-8

1st Printing 1993

Telephone Orders: 1-800-345-1776

Printed in the United States of America

TABLE OF CONTENTS

PART 3 / ARRIVAL:
"Dere's No Hidin' Place Down Here"   63

PART 4 / CONDITIONS OF LIFE:
"We Raise de Wheat, Dey Gib Us de Corn"   69

PART 5 / CHILDHOOD:
"Like a Motherless Child"   85

PART 6 / FAMILY:
"Nobody Knows de Trouble I See"   95

PART 11 / EMANCIPATION: *"The Walls Come Tumblin' Down"*   157

BIBLIOGRAPHY   173

PREFACE

The experience of slavery defies simple generalizations. Novelists like Harriet Beecher Stowe might neatly divide slaves into docile and deferential Uncle Toms and militant and rebellious George Harrises, and masters into brutal and sadistic Simon Legrees and gentle, guilt-ridden Augustine St. Clares. But the realities of slavery were far more complex. Slavery needs to be looked at from the inside, from the perspective of the enslaved. This book tells the story from the perspective of those who experienced it firsthand. Here readers will encounter such famous figures as Frederick Douglass and Nat Turner, as well as many lesser known individuals who will help answer the question: What was it like to be a slave?

This volume is not simply another collection of documents. It begins with a thorough, up-to-date introduction that summarizes what we now know about the history of slavery, the African slave trade, the conditions of slave life, the impact of slavery on the Southern economy, and the process of emancipation.

The introduction is followed by substantial excerpts from published slave narratives, interviews with former slaves, and letters written by enslaved African Americans. Together, these documents draw a comprehensive portrait of slavery. These selections are organized around the concept of the cycle of life under slavery: from memories of growing up in Africa to the trials of the Middle Passage and the horrors of the auction block; then on to the sustaining forces of family and religion, acts of resistance, and the meaning of the Civil War and emancipation. No single person experienced all of these phases of slave life. But all of the enslaved underwent many of these critical experiences.

African American Voices

The Life Cycle of Slavery

INTRODUCTION

Two anecdotes suggest the complex realities of slavery. The first involves a woman listed in the census simply as Celia. She was just fourteen years old in 1850, when a sixty-year-old Missouri farmer named Robert Newsome purchased her. A widower with two grown daughters, Newsome raped Celia before he had even brought her to his farm. For five years he kept her as his sexual slave, forcing her to bear two illegitimate children. In 1855, pregnant a third time and ill, she struck back by hitting her abuser on the head with a club and burning his body in her fireplace. During her murder trial, Celia's attorneys argued that a woman had a right to use deadly force to prevent rape. But the court ruled that in Missouri, as in other slave states, it was not a crime to rape a slave woman. Celia was found guilty and hanged.

The second anecdote involves a Virginia-born slave named Benjamin Montgomery, who was seventeen when a Mississippi planter named Joseph Davis purchased him in 1850. Davis, the elder brother of the Confederate President Jefferson Davis, had previously met the British utopian reformer Robert Owen and wanted to apply Owen's ideas to his own plantation. So he instituted a system of self-government there, including a court system in which slaves ruled on any cases of misconduct, and gave slaves like Benjamin Montgomery access to his personal library. Montgomery educated himself and became a skilled mechanic. He managed the plantation's steam-powered cotton gin and ran a retail store, eventually earning enough money to purchase his family's freedom. As a freedman, he and his family decided to remain on the plantation, and after the Civil War, Montgomery actually bought the property from Davis and ran it until his death in 1877.

Obviously the experience of slavery varied widely, depending on a slaveholder's character and whims. Some masters, like

1

Joseph Davis, attempted to treat their slaves in a kind, paternalistic manner. On the other hand, as Celia's example reveals, the institution of slavery could also bring out the very worst characteristics of human nature by allowing masters to treat human beings as property, to be exploited however they wished.

Slavery in Historical Perspective

During the nineteenth century, slavery was often described as "the peculiar institution." But throughout much of human history, wage labor, not forced labor, was the truly peculiar institution. Most people worked, not out of a desire to better their condition in life, but because they were forced to: as slaves, serfs, peons, or indentured servants.

Slavery began in ancient times. It could be found in societies as diverse as Assyria, Babylonia, China, Egypt, India, Persia, and Mesopotamia; in classical Greece and Rome; in Africa, the Islamic world, and among the New World Indians. While it declined in northwestern Europe after the fall of the Roman Empire, it persisted along the Mediterranean Sea, largely as a result of warfare between Christians and Muslims. Slavery was practiced in eastern Europe and Russia; in North Africa; and in Renaissance Italy, Portugal, and Spain. Linking all these diverse societies was a shared conception of slaves as human beings who could be bought, sold, and exploited as though they were domestic animals.

When Europeans began to colonize the New World at the end of the fifteenth century, they were well aware of the institution of slavery. Europeans used black and Russian slaves to raise sugar on Italian plantations as early as 1300. During the 1400s, decades before Columbus's "discovery" of the New World, Europeans exploited African labor on slave plantations on sugar-producing islands that lay off the West African coast. With European colonization of the New World came a dramatic expansion in slavery. During the sixteenth century, Portugal and Spain extended racial slavery into the New World, opening sugar, coffee, and cotton plantations in Brazil and the West Indies and forcing black slaves in Mexico to work in mines. During the seventeenth century, England, France, Denmark, and Holland established slavery in their New World colonies.

Was the slavery that developed in the New World different from the kinds of servitude found in classical antiquity or in other societies? In one respect New World slavery clearly was not unique. Slavery everywhere permitted cruelty and abuse. Consider these examples: In Homer's Greece, it was not a crime for a master to beat or kill a slave, and the testimony of unskilled slaves was not allowed in court unless it was obtained through torture. Vedius Pollio, a citizen of Rome, reportedly fed the bodies of his slaves to his pet fish. Flavius Gratianus, a fourth century Roman emperor, ruled that any slave who dared accuse his master of a crime should be immediately burned alive. Roman slaves who participated in revolts were crucified on crosses. In ancient India, Saxon England, and ancient China, a master might mistreat or even kill a slave with impunity. Aztec Mexico publicly staged the ritual torture and killing of slaves.

Yet in other fundamental aspects New World slavery differed from slavery in classical antiquity and in Africa, eastern and central Asia, or the Middle East. For one thing, slavery in the classical and the early medieval worlds was not based on racial distinctions. In the ancient world, slavery had nothing to do with the color of a person's skin. In ancient Rome, for example, the slave population included Ethiopians, Gauls, Jews, Persians, and Scandinavians. Unlike seventeenth, eighteenth, or nineteenth century Europeans, the people of the ancient world placed no premium on racial purity and attached no stigma upon racial mixture. Ancient societies, however, did tattoo, brand, or mutilate their slaves as a symbol of their debased status.

Racial slavery originated during the Middle Ages, when Christians and Muslims increasingly began to recruit slaves from East, North-central, and West Africa. As late as the fifteenth century, slavery did not automatically mean black slavery. Many slaves—both in southern Europe and in the Islamic world—came from the Crimea, the Balkans, and the steppes of Western Asia. But after 1453, when the Ottoman Turks captured Constantinople, the capital of Eastern Christendom, and began to monopolize the supply of "white" slaves, Christian slave traders drew increasingly upon captive black Muslims, known as Moors, and upon slaves purchased on the West African coast or transported across the Sahara Desert. By the eighteenth century, Islamic societies also became dependent almost exclusively on sub-Saharan African slaves. Thus the most menial, arduous, and degrading forms of labor became associated with black slaves.

Apart from its racial basis, another distinction between modern and ancient slavery was that the ancient world did not necessarily regard slavery as a permanent condition. In many societies, slaves were allowed to marry free spouses and become members of their owners' families. In ancient Babylonia, for instance, freeborn women and male slaves frequently married, and their children were considered to be free. Access to freedom tended to be far easier under ancient slavery than it was under American slavery. In Greece and Rome, manumission of slaves—giving them their freedom—was not uncommon, and former slaves carried little stigma from their previous status.

A third key difference between ancient and modern slavery was that slaves did not necessarily hold the lowest status in pre-modern societies. While we today draw a sharp distinction between slavery and wage labor, such a distinction was largely non-existent in the world of classical antiquity. Slaves could be among the wealthiest or most influential people in a city. The Bible, for example, tells the story of Joseph, who after being sold into slavery by his brothers, became a trusted governor, counselor, and administrator in Egypt. In classical Greece, many educators, scholars, poets, and physicians were in fact slaves. And in ancient Rome, slaves ranged from those who labored in mines to many merchants and urban craftsmen. In the ancient Near East, slaves could conduct trade and business on their own for their masters. In certain Muslim societies, rulers were customarily recruited among the sons of female slaves.

Finally, it was only in the New World that slavery provided the labor force for a high-pressure, profit-making, capitalist system of plantation agriculture producing cotton, sugar, coffee, and cocoa for distant markets. While many slaves in the ancient world toiled in mines and agricultural fields or on construction and irrigation projects, and suffered extremely high death rates, it appears that ancient slavery was primarily a household institution. In general, ancient peoples did not breed slaves or subject them to the kind of regimented efficiency found on slave plantations in the West Indies or the American South. It appears that most slaves in Africa, in the Islamic world, and in the New World prior to European colonization, worked as farmers or household servants, or served as concubines or eunuchs. They were symbols of prestige, luxury, and power rather than a source of labor. Under modern New World slavery, slaves became the dominant labor force in plantation agriculture.

The Atlantic Slave Trade

African slaves played a critical role in the settlement and economic development of the New World. Enslaved Africans arrived in the New World at least as early as 1502. And over the next three centuries, European slave traders shipped to the West approximately 11.7 million Africans. (Islamic traders probably exported an equal number into North Africa, Arabia, Yemen, Iraq, Iran, and India). Nearly 2 million slaves died during the infamous Middle Passage across the Atlantic to the Americas, a trip that usually took more than seven weeks. During the peak years of the slave trade, between 1740 and 1810, Africa supplied 60,000 captives a year—outnumbering Europeans migrating to the New World.

By the beginning of the eighteenth century, black slaves could be found in every New World area colonized by Europeans from Nova Scotia to Argentina. While the concentrations of slave labor were greatest in England's southern colonies, the Caribbean, and Latin America, where slaves were employed in mines or on sugar, rice, tobacco, and cotton plantations, slaves were also put to work in Northern seaports and on commercial farms. In 1690, one out of every nine families in Boston owned a slave. In New York City in 1703, the proportion was even higher. There, two out of every five families owned a slave.

How did the slave traders get their "merchandise"? African slaves were often captured in tribal wars or in surprise raids on villages. Adults were bound and gagged and infants were sometimes thrown into sacks. One of the earliest first-hand accounts of the African slave trade comes from a seaman named Gomes Eannes de Azurara, who witnessed a Portuguese raid on an African village. He said that some captives "drowned themselves in the water; others thought to escape by hiding under their huts; others shoved their children among the sea-weed."

After capture, the captives were bound together at the neck and marched barefoot, sometimes hundreds of miles, to the Atlantic coast. African captives typically suffered death rates of 20 percent or more while being marched overland. Observers reported seeing hundreds of skeletons along the slave caravan routes. At the coast, the captives were held in pens (known as barracoons) guarded by dogs. Here the captives who survived the forced march to the sea were then examined by European slave traders: "The Countenance and Stature, a good Set of Teeth, Pliancy in the Limbs and Joints, and being free of Venereal Taint, are the things inspected and governs our choice in buying," wrote one slave trader. Those who were bought were branded, assigned numbers, and forced aboard ships; the others were simply abandoned.

Once on shipboard, slaves were chained together and crammed into spaces sometimes less than five feet high. One observer said that slaves were packed together "like books upon a shelf . . . so close that the shelf would not easily contain one more." The death rate on these slave ships was very high—reaching 25 percent in the seventeenth and early eighteenth centuries and remaining around 10 percent in the nineteenth century—as a result of malnutrition and such diseases as dysentery, measles, scurvy, and smallpox.

Many Africans resisted enslavement. On shipboard, slaves were known to mutiny, attempt suicide, jump overboard, or refuse to eat. To prevent their captives from starving themselves, slave traders sometimes smashed out their teeth and fed them by force. To prevent their escape, some captains actually cut off the arms and legs of a few kidnapped Africans.

Upon arrival in the New World, enslaved Africans underwent the final stage in the process of enslavement, a rigorous process known as "seasoning." Many slaves died of disease or suicide, but other African captives conspired to escape slavery by running away and forming "maroon" colonies in remote parts of South Carolina, Florida, Brazil, Guiana, and Jamaica, and Surinam.

Apologists for the African slave trade long argued that European traders did not enslave anyone: they simply purchased Africans who had already been enslaved and who otherwise would have been put to death. Thus, apologists claimed, the slave trade actually saved lives. Such claims are a gross misrepresentation of the facts. Some independent slave merchants did in fact stage raids on unprotected African villages and kidnap and enslave Africans. Most professional slave traders, however, set up bases along the West African coast where they purchased slaves from Africans in exchange for firearms and other goods. Before the end of the seventeenth century, England, France, Denmark, Holland, and Portugal had all established slave trading posts on the West African coast.

Yet to simply say that Europeans purchased people who had already been enslaved is a serious distortion of historical reality. While there had been a slave trade within Africa prior to the arrival of Europeans, the massive European demand for slaves and the introduction of firearms radically transformed West African society. A growing number of Africans were enslaved for petty debts or minor criminal or religious offenses or as victims in unprovoked raids on unprotected villages. European weapons certainly made it easier to capture slaves.

Some African societies, like Benin in southern Nigeria, refused to sell slaves. Others, like Dahomey, appear to have spe-

cialized in selling them. Still other societies, like Asante, in present-day Ghana, and the Yoruba, in Western Nigeria, engaged in
wars that produced as many as half of all eighteenth and early
nineteenth century slaves.

The slave trade also had profound effects on Europe. Between
the early 1500s and the early 1800s, the slave trade became one of
Europe's largest and most profitable industries. Profits from the
slave trade were said to run as high as 300 percent. In the mid-
eighteenth century, a third of the British merchant fleet was
engaged in transporting 50,000 Africans a year to the New World.

But it was not just slave traders or New World planters who
benefited from the slave trade. American shipowners, farmers, and
fisherman also profited from slavery. Slavery played a central role
in the growth of commercial capitalism in the colonies. While the
slave plantations of the West Indies became the largest market for
American fish, oats, corn, flour, lumber, peas, beans, hogs, and
horses, New Englanders distilled molasses produced by slaves in
the French and Dutch West Indies into rum.

Although slavery did not create a major share of the capital
that financed Europe's industrial revolution (profits from the slave
trade and New World plantations did not add up to five percent of
Britain's national income at the beginning of the industrial revolution), slave labor did produce the major consumer goods that were
the basis of world trade during the seventeenth, eighteenth, and
early nineteenth centuries: coffee, cotton, rum, sugar, and tobacco.
In addition, the slave trade provided stimulus to shipbuilding,
banking, and insurance; and Africa became a major market for
iron, textiles, firearms, and rum.

The Origins of New World Slavery

Why did Spanish, Portuguese, French, Dutch, Danish, and
English colonists all bring slaves to their New World colonies?
Few questions have aroused more heated debate than the origins
of New World slavery. Was it, as some have argued, the product of
deep-seated racial prejudice? Or was it the product of a haphazard
and random process that gradually occurred with little thought
about the ultimate outcome? Or were other forces at work?

Certainly there is a great deal of evidence showing that
sixteenth-century Europeans held deeply racist sentiments well
before the establishment of black slavery. We know, for example,
that the Elizabethan English associated blackness with evil, death,

and danger. They portrayed the devil as having black skin and associated beauty with fair skin. Through their religion, the English denigrated people of color, claiming that Negroes were the descendants of Noah's son Ham who was cursed by having black offspring for daring to look upon his drunken and naked father. Long before the English had contact with Africa, racist stereotypes were widespread. One English writer claimed that Negroes were naturally "addicted unto Treason, Treacherie, Murther, Theft and Robberie." Without a doubt, it was easy for the English to accept slavery because they regarded Negroes as an alien people.

But there was nothing inevitable about New World colonists relying on an enslaved black labor force. At first, Europeans sought to enslave Indians. Within a century, however, the Indian population declined by 50 to 90 percent, mainly as a result of European-introduced diseases. So the European colonists had to consider other sources of labor.

Initially, colonists in every English colony relied on indentured white servants rather than on black slaves. During the late fifteenth and early sixteenth centuries, England's population grew by over a third, much faster than its economy. To address a sudden explosion of crime and poverty, England's rulers forced the poor to toil in workhouses, and beginning in 1547 enslaved persistent vagabonds and branded them with the letter "S."

In the early 1600s, England came to view New World colonization as a providential solution to the country's problem of overpopulation. Thousands of England's unemployed and underemployed farmers, urban laborers, debtors, and criminals were sent as "indentured servants" to the New World, where they contributed to England's wealth by raising tobacco and producing other goods. Over half of all white immigrants to the English colonies during the seventeenth century consisted of convicts or indentured servants.

In becoming an indentured servant, a person agreed to work for a four or five year term of service in return for transportation to the New World as well as food, clothing, and shelter. In certain respects, the status of white servitude differed little from that of slavery. Like slaves, servants could be bought, sold, or leased. They could also be punished by whipping. Unlike slaves, however, servants were allowed to own property, and, when their term of service was finished (if they indeed survived—many did not), they received their freedom along with small sums of money known as "freedom dues."

Black slavery took root in the American colonies slowly. As early as 1619, a Dutch ship carried the first Africans to Virginia, but it would not be until the 1680s that black slavery became the dominant labor system on plantations there. As late as 1640, there were probably only 150 blacks in Virginia (the colony with the highest black population), and in 1650, 300. But by 1680, the number had risen to 3,000 and by 1704, to 10,000. Faced by a shortage of white indentured servants and fearful of servant revolt, English settlers increasingly resorted to enslaved Africans.

Toward Slavery

Anthony Johnson was one of Virginia's first slaves. Arriving in 1621, he was put to work on a plantation along the James River, where he took a wife, Mary, and raised at least four children. During the 1630s, Johnson and his family gained their freedom, probably by purchasing it themselves. Johnson subsequently acquired an estate of 250 acres, which he farmed with the help of white indentured servants and at least one slave. Just as remarkably, Johnson successfully sued in court for the return of a slave, who he claimed had been stolen by two white neighbors.

As Johnson's life suggests, the black experience in seventeenth century America was extremely complex. Some blacks were permanently unfree; others, were treated like white indentured servants. They were allowed to own property and to marry and were freed after a term of service. A few slaves, like Francis Payne who lived in Eastern Virginia, were assigned plots of land remote from their master's homes and were allowed to raise tobacco and other crops and purchase their own freedom. In several cases, black slaves who could prove that they had been baptized successfully sued for their freedom. In one Eastern Virginia county in 1668, 29 percent of all blacks were free.

As early as the late 1630s, however, the English colonists began to make a distinction between the status of white servants and black slaves. In 1639, Maryland became the first colony to specifically state that baptism as a Christian did not make a slave a free person. Discrimination against black servants began to increase. In 1640, when two white indentured servants and a black indentured servant named John Punch fled from Virginia to Maryland, all three received thirty lashes. The whites also had their terms of service extended by four years; but Punch was condemned to lifelong servitude. In 1669, Virginia became the first colony to declare that it was not a crime to kill an unruly slave in the ordinary course of punishment.

As the slave population grew in size, racial lines grew increasingly rigid. By the end of the seventeenth century, Virginia and Maryland had forbidden interracial marriages and sexual relations. Laws adopted in several colonies in the early eighteenth century confiscated slaves' property, forbade masters from freeing their slaves, permitted masters to mutilate and dismember disobedient slaves, and declared that slave status was inherited through the mother. The law now defined Africans as chattel property, unprotected by any legal system.

To meet planters' growing demand for slaves, the English government established the Royal African Company in 1672. After 1698, when Britain ended the Royal African Company's monopoly of the slave trade, the number of enslaved Africans brought into the colonies soared. Between 1700 and 1775, more than 350,000 Africans slaves entered the American colonies. By the mid-eighteenth century, blacks made up almost 70 percent of the population of South Carolina, 40 percent in Virginia, 8 percent in Pennsylvania, and 4 percent in New England.

Much of the increase in the size of the slave population was the result of natural reproduction. During the seventeenth century, slaves had had few opportunities to establish stable family relationships. In the Chesapeake colonies and the Carolinas, two-thirds of all slaves were male, and most slaves lived on plantations with fewer than ten slaves. These units were so small and widely dispersed and the sex ratio was so skewed that it was difficult for slaves to find spouses. A high death rate meant that many slaves did not live long enough to marry or, if they did, their marriages did not last very long.

Beginning in the 1720s, however, slaves in the Chesapeake region became the first slave population in the New World able to reproduce their own numbers. As late as the early nineteenth century, slave mortality in the Caribbean exceeded slave fertility by two to five percent a year, meaning that the West Indian slave population would rapidly decline in the absence of slave importation. In the United States, the slave population tripled after the end of the African slave trade.

Antebellum Slavery

During the last years of the eighteenth century, New World slavery seemed to be declining. As a result of the American and French revolutions, thousands of black slaves escaped slavery through revolt or simply by running away. Revolutionary ideals of liberty and equality encouraged many slaveowners in the United States, the Caribbean, and Spanish America to emancipate their slaves. In the ten years after Virginia enacted a law allowing private manumissions, Virginian masters freed 10,000 slaves. A French traveler observed that people throughout the South "are constantly talking of abolishing slavery, of contriving some other means of cultivating their estates."

But slavery was not, in fact, on the road to extinction. During the early nineteenth century, slavery underwent a new boom, rapidly expanding in Brazil, Cuba, Trinidad, Guiana, the Windward Islands, and new territories south and west of the Appalachian mountains in the United States: into Georgia, Alabama, Mississippi, Louisiana, Arkansas, Missouri, and Texas.

Eli Whitney's invention of the cotton gin gave a new thrust to slavery. Between 1792, when Whitney invented the cotton gin, and 1794, the price of slaves doubled. By 1825, field hands, who had brought $500 apiece in 1794, were worth $1,500. As the price of slaves inflated, so, too, did their numbers. During the first decade of the nineteenth century, the number of slaves in the United States rose by 33 percent; during the following decade, the slave population grew another 29 percent.

What Was Life Like Under Slavery?

Prior to the Civil War, abolitionists charged that slaves were overworked, poorly clad, inadequately housed, and cruelly punished; that slavery was a highly profitable investment; and that far from being content, slaves longed for freedom. Apologists for slavery, in turn, accused abolitionists of exaggerating slavery's evils, asserting that slaves were rarely whipped, that marriages were seldom broken by sale, and that most slaves were able to maintain stable family lives. They maintained that paternalism and public opinion protected slaves from cruelty; that slave insurrections were rare because most slaves were content with bondage; that slavery was an economic burden that planters bore out of a sense of responsibility; and that slaves enjoyed a higher standard of living, a better diet, superior housing, and a greater life expectancy than many free urban workers in the North and in Europe.

Recent historical research has largely confirmed the abolitionist indictment of slavery. We now know that slaves suffered extremely high mortality. Half of all slave infants died during their first year of life, twice the rate of white babies. And while the death rate declined for those who survived their first year, it still remained twice the white rate through age 14. As a result of this high infant and childhood mortality rate, the average life expectancy of a slave at birth was just 21 to 22 years, compared to 40 to 43 years for antebellum whites.

A major contributor to the high infant and child death rate was chronic undernourishment. Slaveowners showed such little concern for slave mothers' health or diet during pregnancy, providing pregnant women with no extra rations and employing them in intensive field work even in the last week before they gave birth. Not surprisingly, slave mothers suffered high rates of spontaneous abortions, stillbirths, and deaths shortly after birth. Half of all slave infants weighed less than 5.5 pounds at birth, or what we would today consider to be severely underweight.

Infants and children were badly malnourished. Most infants were weaned early, within three or four months of birth, and then fed gruel or porridge made of cornmeal. Around the age of three, they began to eat vegetables, soups, potatoes, molasses, grits, hominy, and cornbread. This diet lacked protein, thiamine, niacin, calcium, magnesium, and vitamin D. As a result, slave children often suffered from night blindness, abdominal swellings, swollen muscles, bowed legs, skin lesions, and convulsions. These symptoms apparently stemmed from beriberi, pellagra, tetany, rickets, and kwashiorkor, diseases that are caused by protein and vitamin deficiencies.

Squalid living conditions also contributed to health problems. Chickens, dogs, and pigs lived next to the slave quarters and, consequently, animal feces contaminated the area. Lacking privies, slaves had to urinate and defecate in the cover of nearby bushes. Such squalor contributed to high rates of diarrhea, dysentery, whooping cough, respiratory diseases, hepatitis, typhoid fever, and intestinal worms.

Deprived of an adequate diet, slave children were very small by modern standards. Their average height at age three was shorter than 99 percent of twentieth-century American three-year-olds. At age 17, slave men were shorter than 96 percent of present-day 17-year-old men and slave women were shorter than 80 percent of contemporary women.

Slave Labor

For the vast majority of slaves, slavery meant back-breaking field work: planting, cultivating, and harvesting cotton, hemp, rice, tobacco, or sugar cane. On a typical plantation, slaves worked ten or more hours a day, "from day clean to first dark," six days a week, with only the Sabbath off. At planting or harvesting time, planters required slaves to stay in the fields 15 or 16 hours a day. When they were not raising a cash crop, slaves grew other crops, such as corn or potatoes; cared for livestock; and cleared fields, cut wood, and repaired buildings and fences.

On cotton, sugar, and tobacco plantations, slaves worked together in gangs, their work being supervised by a white overseer or a black driver. On many rice and hemp plantations and the coastal areas of South Carolina and Georgia, slaveowners adopted the task system. Slaves had specific daily work assignments, and after they completed their tasks, their time was their own.

Slave masters extracted labor from virtually the entire slave community, young, old, healthy, and physically impaired. Around the age of three or four, slave children were put to work, usually in special "thrash gangs" weeding fields. Between the ages of seven and twelve, boys and girls were put to work in intensive field work. Older or physically handicapped slaves were put to work in cloth houses—spinning cotton, weaving cloth, and making clothes. Altogether, masters forced two-thirds of all slaves to work—twice the labor force participation rate among the free population, reflecting the high proportion of children, women, and elderly toiling in cotton or rice fields.

Because slaves had no direct incentive to work hard, slaveowners combined harsh penalties with positive incentives. Some masters denied passes for traveling to disobedient slaves. Other confined recalcitrant slaves to private jails. Chains and shackles were widely used to control runaways. Whipping was a key part of plantation discipline. On one Louisiana plantation, a slave was lashed every four-and-a-half days. But physical pain was not the only method used to elicit hard work. To stimulate productivity, some masters gave slaves small garden plots and permitted them to sell their produce. Some distributed gifts of food or money at the end of the year. Still other planters awarded prizes, holidays, and year-end bonuses to particularly productive slaves.

Not all slaves were field hands. During the 1850s, half a million slaves lived in Southern towns and cities where they worked in textile mills, iron works, tobacco factories, laundries, and shipyards. Other slaves labored as lumberjacks, as deckhands on riverboats, and in sawmills, gristmills, and quarries. Many slaves were engaged in construction of roads and railroads. Even on plantations, not all slaves were field laborers. About 250,000 were craftsmen such as blacksmiths, shoemakers, or carpenters or held domestic posts such as coachmen or house servants.

Slave Family and Cultural Life

Under Southern state laws, slaves were considered chattel property. Like a domestic animal, they could be bought, sold, leased, and physically punished. Slaves were prohibited from owning property, testifying against whites in court, or traveling without a pass. Also, their marriages lacked legal sanction. During the nineteenth century, in response to abolitionist attacks on slavery, Southern legislatures enacted laws setting minimal standards for housing, food, and clothing. These statutes, however, were largely ignored and unenforced.

Although some masters, like George Washington, were reluctant to buy or sell slaves, economic need or an owner's death often led to the separation of husbands from wives and parents from children. The most conservative estimates indicate that at least 10 to 20 percent of slave marriages were severed by sale. And even more common was the sale of slave children. Over the course of a 35-year lifespan, a slave had a 50-50 chance of being sold at least once and was likely to witness the sale of several members of his or her immediate family.

Slave families were extremely vulnerable to separation. As a result of the sale or death of a father or mother, over a third of all slave children grew up in households from which one or both parents were absent. About a quarter of all slave children grew up in a single-parent household (nearly always with their mother) and another tenth grew up apart from both parents.

Even in instances in which marriages were not broken by sale, slave spouses often resided on separate plantations, owned by different individuals. On large plantations, one slave father in three had a different owner from his wife, and could visit his wife and family only at his master's discretion. On smaller holdings, divided ownership and mother-headed households occurred even more frequently. Just one-third of the children on farms or plantations with 15 or fewer slaves lived in a two-parent family, compared to two-thirds of the children on larger plantations.

Because many planters prohibited marriages across plantations (and because slaves, like West Africans but unlike white Southerners, would not marry first cousins), many slaves were unable to find a spouse. On the largest plantations, nearly 20 percent of the slaves who reached adulthood remained single throughout their lives.

Other obstacles also stood in the way of an independent family life. Many slaves had to share their single room cabins with relatives or, sometimes, other unrelated slaves. Even on model plantations, children between the ages of seven and 10 were taken from their parents and sent to live in separate cabins.

Slavery severely circumscribed the authority of slave parents. When a slave child named Jacob Stroyer was regularly beaten, his father told him: "Go back to your work and be a good boy, for I cannot do anything for you."

Of all the threats to slave family life, one of the most terrible was the sexual abuse of slave women. Some masters, like James H. Hammond, a congressman, governor, and U.S. senator from South Carolina, took slave mistresses and concubines. Hammond, whose wife bore him eight children, purchased an 18-year-old slave named Sally and her infant daughter, Louisa, in 1839. He made Sally his mistress, and fathered several children by her; and then when her daughter, Louisa reached the age of 12, fathered several children by her. Nor was Hammond singular. Governor Francis Pickens of South Carolina and Confederate General Jubal Early each took slave mistresses. One ex-slave remembered that his master "would ship ... husbands out of bed and get in with their wives." A survey of former slaves conducted in the 1930s revealed that 4.5 percent said that one of their parents had been white.

Despite the frequent breakup of families by sale, African-Americans managed to forge strong and durable family and kin ties within the institution of slavery. In spite of the refusal of southern law to recognize the legality of slave marriages, most slaves married and lived with the same spouse until death, and most slave children grew up in two-parent households.

To sustain a sense of family identity, slaves often named their children after parents, grandparents, recently deceased relatives, and other kin. Slaves also passed down family names to their children, usually the name of an ancestor's owner rather than their current owner's. The strength of slave families is nowhere more evident than in the advertisements slaveowners posted for runaway slaves. Over a third of the advertisements indicate that fugitives left an owner to visit a spouse, a child, or other relatives.

Ties to an immediate family stretched outward to an involved network of extended kin. Family destruction and dispersal created extended kinship networks stretching across whole counties. Whenever children were sold to neighboring plantations, grandparents, aunts, uncles, and cousins often took on the functions of parents. When blood relatives were not present, strangers cared for and protected children. Slave parents taught their children to call all adult slaves "aunt" or "uncle" and younger slaves as "sister" or "brother." In this way, slave culture taught the young that they were members of a broader community in which all slaves had mutual obligations and responsibilities.

Slave religious and cultural traditions played a particularly important role in helping slaves survive the harshness and misery of life under slavery. In the realms of art, dance, folklore, language, music, and religion, slaves created a distinctive culture which blended African and European elements into a new synthesis.

During the late eighteenth and early nineteenth centuries, slaves embraced Christianity, but transformed it to meet their own needs. Slave religious beliefs, a mixture of Christianity and African traditions, provided slaves with the patience and hope necessary to endure slavery. Slave religion also upheld a vision of the spiritual equality of all human beings that strengthened their hopes of eventual deliverance from bondage. Spirituals, like "Go Down, Moses," with its refrain "let my people go," indicate slaves identified with the Hebrew people who had overcome oppression and enslavement.

Through folklore, slaves also sustained a sense of separate identity and conveyed valuable lessons to their children. Among the most popular folktales were animal trickster stories, like the Brer Rabbit tales, derived from similar African stories, which told of powerless creatures who got even through wit and guile, not power and authority.

American Slavery in Comparative Perspective

Most African slaves were shipped not to what is now the United States but to Brazil and the West Indies. Of the nearly 10 million Africans who survived the voyage to the New World, over a third landed in Brazil and between 60 and 70 percent ended up in Brazil or the sugar colonies of the Caribbean. Just 6 percent of African slaves were imported into the American colonies. Yet by 1860, two-thirds of all New World slaves lived in the American South.

How did American slavery compare and contrast with slavery in Latin America and the Caribbean? Was it more repressive or was it more benign? For a long time it was widely assumed that

Southern slavery was harsher and crueler than slavery in Latin America, where the Catholic Church insisted that slaves had a right to marry, to seek relief from a cruel master, and to purchase their freedom. In contrast to the American South, it was pointed out, there was no legal prohibition in Latin America on educating or freeing a slave. Moreover, Spanish and Portuguese colonists were thought to be less tainted by racial prejudice than North Americans, and Latin American slavery was believed to be less subject to the pressures of a competitive capitalist economy.

This contrast between a supposedly kinder, gentler system of Latin American slavery and a harsher system of North American slavery appears to be grossly overdrawn. In practice, neither the Catholic Church nor the courts offered much protection to Latin American slaves. Cruel punishments were not unknown, such as tying slaves down and periodically flogging them for nine to thirteen consecutive days. Slaveowners in Latin America, like those in the American South, frequently sold family members separately. Access to freedom was greater in Latin America; but in many cases masters freed sick, elderly, crippled, or simply unneeded slaves in order to relieve themselves of financial responsibilities. In certain respects, Latin American slavery may have been even harsher than North American slavery. Death rates among slaves in the Caribbean were one-third higher than in the South, and suicide appears to have been much more common. Sometimes Latin American slaves were forced to wear iron masks to keep them from eating dirt or drinking liquor. Unlike slaves in the South, West Indian slaves were expected to produce their own food in their "free time," and care for the elderly and the infirm.

For all the similarities between slavery in the American South and in Latin America, there were a number of crucial differences. Perhaps the most obvious was demographic. The slave population in Brazil and the West Indies had a low proportion of female slaves, a tiny slave birth rate, and a high proportion of recent arrivals from Africa. In striking contrast, Southern slaves had an equal sex ratio, a high birthrate, and a predominantly American-born population. Slaves also made up sharply differing proportions of the total population. In the West Indies, slaves constituted 80 to 90 percent of the population, while in the South only about a third of the population were slaves.

Plantation size also differed widely. In the Caribbean, slaves were held on much larger units, with many plantations holding as many as 500 slaves. In the American South, in contrast, only one slaveowner held as many as a thousand slaves, and half of all slaves in the United States worked on units of twenty or fewer slaves; three-quarters had fewer than fifty.

These demographic differences had important social implications. In the American South, slaveowners lived on their plantations and slaves dealt with their owners regularly. Most planters placed plantation management, supply purchasing, and supervision in the hands of black drivers and foremen, and at least two-thirds of all slaves worked under the supervision of black drivers. In contrast, absentee ownership was far more prevalent in the West Indies, where planters relied heavily on paid managers and relied on a distinct class of free blacks and mulattoes to serve as intermediaries with the slave population. Standards of diet, housing, and medicine in the South may have exceeded those in the Caribbean, but Southern masters also interfered more frequently in their slaves' personal lives. In the South, masters provided slaves with food, housing, and clothing; in the Caribbean, in contrast, slaves had to raise their own food in their spare time.

Another important difference between Latin America and the United States involved the very concept of race. In Spanish and Portuguese America, an intricate system of racial classification emerged. Compared to the British and French, the Spanish and Portuguese were much more tolerant of racial mixing (an attitude encouraged by a shortage of European women) and recognized a wide range of racial gradations, including black, mestizo, quadroon, and octoroon.

The American South, in contrast, adopted a two-category system of racial categorization in which any person with a black mother was automatically considered to be black. It has been said, half-facetiously, that Southerners are color blind, in the sense that individuals, despite their racial composition, are considered to be either white or black, while Latin Americans recognized degrees of blackness and whiteness.

Slave Revolts

While slave masters in the South, Brazil, and the West Indies described their slave population as faithful, docile, and contented, slaveowners always feared slave revolt. One historian has identified over 200 examples of open rebellion or fears of slave conspiracies in America between the early seventeenth and the mid-nineteenth centuries.

Probably the first slave revolt erupted in Hispaniola in 1522. During the early eighteenth century there were slave uprisings in Long Island in 1708 and in New York City in 1712. Slaves in South Carolina staged several insurrections, culminating in the Stono Rebellion in 1739, when they seized firearms, killed whites, and burned houses. In 1740 and 1741, conspiracies were uncovered in Charleston and New York. During the late eighteenth century, slave revolts erupted in Guadeloupe, Grenada, Jamaica, Surinam, San Domingue (Haiti), Venezuela, and the Windward Islands. Many fugitive slaves, known as maroons, fled to remote regions and carried on guerrilla warfare.

During the early nineteenth century, major conspiracies or revolts against slavery took place in Richmond, Virginia, in 1800; in Louisiana in 1811; in Barbados in 1816; in Charleston, South Carolina, in 1822; in Demerara in 1823; and in Jamaica and Southampton County, Virginia, in 1831.

Black religion was instrumental in encouraging resistance to slavery. When Denmark Vesey sought to gain recruits for his plot to overthrow slavery in Charleston in 1822, one slave said, "he [Vesey] tries to prove . . . that slavery and bondage is against the Bible." Nat Turner's 1831 insurrection was inspired by a religious vision that revealed that "the time was fast approaching when the first should be last and the last should be first."

The main result of slave insurrections, throughout the Americas, was the mass executions of blacks. After a slave conspiracy was uncovered in New York City in 1740, 18 slaves were hanged and 13 were burned alive. After Denmark Vesey's conspiracy was uncovered, the authorities in Charleston hanged 37 blacks. Following Nat Turner's insurrection, the local militia killed about 100 blacks and 20 more slaves, including Turner, were later executed. In the South, the preconditions for successful rebellion did not exist, and tended to bring increased suffering and repression to the slave community.

Violent rebellion was rarer and smaller in scale in the American South than in Brazil or the Caribbean, reflecting the relatively small proportion of blacks in the Southern population, the low proportion of recent migrants from Africa, and the relatively small size of Southern plantations. Compared to the Caribbean, prospects for successful, sustained rebellions in the American South were bleak. In Jamaica, slaves outnumbered whites by ten or eleven to one; in the South, a much larger white population was committed to suppressing rebellion. In general, African-born slaves were more likely than New World-born slaves to participate in outright revolts. Not only did many Africans have combat experience prior to enslavement, but they also had fewer family and communities ties that might inhibit violent insurrection.

If outright rebellion occurred less frequently in the South, there were still many examples of passive and active resistance to slavery. Most African-Americans resisted the dehumanizing effects of slavery in a variety of subtle ways. The most common forms of resistance to slavery involved breaking tools, feigning illness, lying, doing shoddy work, and stealing, as well as infanticide, arson, poisoning, sabotage, and murder. One North Carolina cook later recalled that "many times I spit in the biscuits and peed in the coffee just to get back at them mean white folks."

The Economics of Slavery

During the years before the Civil War many Northerners charged that slavery was incompatible with rapid economic growth. Despite clear evidence that slavery was profitable for individual planters, a growing number of people felt that slavery was inherently wasteful and inefficient, that it degraded labor, inhibited urbanization and mechanization, thwarted industrialization, and stifled progress. They associated slavery with economic backwardness, soil exhaustion, low labor productivity, indebtedness, and economic and social stagnation. Philosopher and poet Ralph Waldo Emerson said that "slavery is no scholar, no improver . . . it does not increase the white population; it does not improve the soil; everything goes to decay."

Like other slave societies, the South did not produce urban centers on a scale equal with those in the North. Virginia's largest city, Richmond, had a population of just 15,274 in 1850. That same year, Wilmington—North Carolina's largest city—had just 7,264 inhabitants. Southern cities were small because they failed to develop diversified economies. Unlike the cities of the North, Southern cities rarely became centers of commerce, finance, or processing and manufacturing and southern ports rarely engaged in international trade.

By northern standards, the South's transportation network was primitive. Traveling the 1,460 miles from Baltimore to New Orleans in 1850 meant riding five different railroads, two stage coaches, and two steamboats. Its educational system also lagged far behind the North's. In 1850, 20 percent of adult white southerners could not read or write, compared to a national figure of 8 percent.

Does this mean that slavery was a waning institution? Was it doomed to extinction, even without a Civil War? The answer appears to be "no." Although in 1860 the South didn't compare to the North, the South was still more prosperous than any European nation except England, and had a higher per capita income than Italy on the eve of World War II.

Slave labor was efficient, productive, and adaptable to a variety of occupations, ranging from agriculture and mining to factory work. Slavery was the basis of the nation's most profitable industry. During the decades before the Civil War, slave grown cotton accounted for over half the value of all United States exports, and provided virtually all the cotton used in the northern textile industry and 70 percent of the cotton used in British mills. Furthermore, a disproportionate share of the richest Americans made their fortunes from slavery. In 1860, two out of every three Americans worth $100,000 or more lived in the South.

Nevertheless, the South's political leaders had good reason for concern. Within the South, slave ownership was becoming concentrated into a fewer number of hands. The proportion of Southern families owning slaves declined from 36 percent in 1830 to 25 percent in 1860. At the same time, slavery was sharply declining in the upper South. Between 1830 and 1860, the proportion of slaves in Missouri's population fell from 18 to 10 percent; in Kentucky, from 24 to 19 percent; in Maryland, from 23 to 13 percent. By the middle of the nineteenth century, slavery was becoming an oddity in the New World, confined to Brazil, Cuba, Puerto Rico, a number of small Dutch colonies, and the American South. In the American South the most powerful threat to ending slavery came from abolitionists, who denounced slavery as immoral.

Abolition

The growth of public opposition to slavery represents one of the most momentous moral transformations in history. As late as 1750, no church condemned slave ownership or slave trading. Britain, Denmark, France, Holland, Portugal, and Spain all openly participated in the slave trade. Beginning with the Quakers in the late 1750s, however, organized opposition to slavery quickly grew. In 1787, the Northwest Ordinance barred slavery from the territories north of the Ohio River; by 1804, all nine states north of Delaware had freed their slaves or adopted gradual emancipation plans. In 1807, the United States and Britain outlawed the African slave trade.

The wars of national liberation in Spanish America ended slavery in Spain's mainland New World empire. In 1821, the region that now includes Ecuador, Colombia, and Venezuela adopted a gradual emancipation plan. Two years later, Chile agreed to emancipate its slaves, and in 1829, Mexico did the same.

In 1833, Britain emancipated 780,000 slaves, paying 20 million pounds sterling compensation to their owners. In 1848, Denmark and France freed slaves in their colonial empires. Slavery survived in Surinam and other Dutch New World colonies until 1863 and in the United States until 1865. The last New World slaves were emancipated in Cuba in 1886 and in Brazil in 1888.

Within the span of a century and a half, slavery, long regarded as an integral part of the social order, came to be seen as a violation of Christian morality and the natural, inalienable rights of man. The main impetus behind antislavery came from religion. New religious and humanitarian values contributed to a view of slavery as "the sum of all villainies," a satanic institution which gave rise to every imaginable sin: violence, despotism, racial prejudice, and sexual corruption.

Initially, many opponents of slavery supported "colonization"—the deportation of black Americans to Africa, the Caribbean, or Central America. But by the late 1820s, it was obvious that colonization was a wholly impractical solution to the problem of slavery. Where the nation's slave population rose by 50,000 every year, in 1830, the American Colonization Society could persuade only 259 free blacks to migrate to Liberia, bringing the total number of blacks colonized in Africa to just 1,400.

In 1829, a twenty-five-year-old white Bostonian named William Lloyd Garrison denounced colonization as a cruel hoax designed to promote the racial purity of the North while doing nothing to end slavery in the South. He demanded "immediate emancipation" of slaves without compensation to their owners. Within six years, 200 antislavery societies had sprouted up in the North, and had mounted a massive propaganda campaign against slavery.

The growth of militant abolitionism sometimes provoked a harsh public reaction. Mobs led by "gentlemen of property and standing" attacked the homes and businesses of abolitionist merchants, destroyed abolitionist printing presses, attacked black neighborhoods, and murdered the Reverend Elijah P. Lovejoy, the editor of an abolitionist newspaper. In the face of vicious attacks, the antislavery movement divided over questions of strategy and tactics. Radicals, led by Garrison, began to attack all forms of inequality and violence in American society, withdrew from churches that condoned slavery, demanded equal rights for women, and called for voluntary dissolution of the Union. Other abolitionists turned to politics as the most promising way to end slavery, helping to form the Liberty Party in 1840, the Free Soil Party in 1848, and the Republican Party in 1854.

By the late 1850s, a growing number of northerners were convinced that slavery posed an intolerable threat to free labor and civil liberties. Many believed that an aggressive Slave Power had seized control of the federal government, incited revolution in Texas and war with Mexico, and was engaged in a systematic plan to extend slavery into the Western territories. At the same time, an increasing number of southerners believed that antislavery radicals dominated northern politics and sought to bar slavery from the western territories and to undermine the institution in the states where it already existed. John Brown's raid on the federal arsenal at Harpers Ferry in October 1859 produced shockwaves throughout the South, producing fears of slave revolt and race war. When Abraham Lincoln was elected in 1860, many white southerners were convinced that this represented the triumph of abolitionism in the North and thought they had no choice but to secede from the Union. The new president, however, was passionately committed to the preservation of the union, and peaceful secession was not an option.

The Experience of Liberation

Slaves played a pivotal role in their own liberation. During the first two years of the Civil War, federal officials refused to enlist black soldiers in the Union Army. But by early 1863, voluntary enlistments had fallen so sharply that the federal government instituted an unpopular military draft and decided to enroll black, as well as white, troops. Indeed, it was the availability of black troops that allowed President Lincoln to resist demands for a negotiated peace which might have included the retaining of slavery in the United States. Altogether, 186,000 black soldiers served in the Union Army and another 29,000 served in the Navy, accounting for nearly 10 percent of all Union forces and 68,178 of the Union dead or missing. Three-fifths of all black troops were former slaves. The active participation of black troops made it inconceivable that African-Americans would remain in slavery after the Civil War.

While in the army, black troops also faced a different kind of battle: against discrimination in pay, promotions, and medical care. Despite promises of equal treatment, blacks were relegated to separate regiments commanded by white officers. Black soldiers received less pay than white soldiers, inferior benefits, and poorer food and equipment. While a white private was paid $13 a month plus a $3.50 clothing allowance, blacks received just $10 a month, out of which $3 was deducted for clothing. Until the end of the war, the government refused to commission black officers. Within the ranks, black troops faced repeated humiliations; most were employed in menial assignments and kept in rear-echelon, fatigue assignments. Within the Union army, they were punished by whipping, others were tied up by their thumbs; if captured by the Confederates, they faced execution. But despite these trials, black soldiers won the opportunity to fight and the battle for equal pay (in 1864). Drawing upon the education and training they received in the military, many black troops became community leaders during Reconstruction.

During the war, many Southern slaves contributed to their own emancipation by deserting plantations and fleeing to Union lines. Slaves staged a few insurrections during the war as the slave system itself was beginning to unravel. Planters were stunned to see trusted house slaves and field drivers lead field hands in deserting to the Union army.

For ex-slaves, emancipation was a moment of exhilaration, fear, and uncertainty. While some greeted the announcement of freedom with jubilation, others reacted with stunned silence. Thousands of freedmen wandered the South, struggling desperately, but largely unsuccessfully, to reunite families forcibly separated by sale. A northern journalist met an ex-slave in North Carolina who had walked 600 miles searching for his wife and children who had been sold four years before. Many couples, forbidden to marry during slavery, took the opportunity to formalize their unions, while others, who had lived apart from their families on separate plantations, were finally free to reside with their spouses. As an expression of their emancipation, many freedmen changed their slave names, adopted new surnames, and insisted on being addressed as "mister" and "misses." Shocked at seeing former slaves transformed into free women and men, Southern whites complained of "betrayal" and "ingratitude" when the freedmen left their plantations. Revealing slaveowners' capacity for self-deception, one former master complained that "those we loved best, and who loved us best—as we thought—were the first to leave us." In many parts of the South, the end of the war was followed by an outburst of white rage: whites whipped, clubbed, and murdered freed slaves. In contrast, the vast majority of former slaves refrained from vengeance against former masters. Instead, they struggled to achieve social and political independence by forming separate black churches and schools, mutual aid societies, lodges, newspapers, and political organizations.

The Aftermath of Slavery

Except for Haiti, the American South was the only region in the western hemisphere in which slavery was overthrown by force of arms. It was the only region, except for Brazil, in which slave owners received no compensation for the loss of their slave property; and the only region, except for Gaudeloupe and Martinique, in which former slaves received civil and political rights. Furthermore, the American South was the only postemancipation society in which large slaveowners were deprived of the right to hold public office and in which former slaves formed successful political alliances with whites.

Yet, with all these concessions, the abolition of slavery did not mean that former slaves had achieved full freedom. Throughout the western hemisphere, the end of slavery was followed by a period of reconstruction in which race relations were redefined and new systems of labor emerged. In former slave societies throughout the Americas, ex-slaves sought to free themselves from the gang system of labor on plantations and establish small-scale, self-sufficient farms, while planters and local governments sought to restore the plantation system. The outcome, in many former slave societies, was the emergence of a caste system of race relations and a system of involuntary or forced labor such as peonage, debt bondage, apprenticeship, contract laborers, indentured laborers, tenant farming, and sharecropping.

In every postemancipation society, the abolition of slavery resulted in acute labor problems and declining productivity, spurring efforts to restore plantation discipline. Even in Haiti, where black revolution had overthrown slavery, repeated attempts were made to restore the plantation system. On Caribbean islands like Barbados where land was totally controlled by whites, the plantation system was reimposed. In other areas, like Jamaica, where former slaves were able to squat on unsettled land and set up subsistence farms, staple production fell sharply. To counteract a sharp decline in sugar production, the British government imported thousands of "coolie" laborers from Asia into the Caribbean. To force former ex-slaves to work on plantations, Caribbean governments enacted regressive taxes and strict vagrancy laws.

The story of Reconstruction in the American South echoes a broad concern about labor control. Immediately following the war, all-white Southern legislatures passed "black codes" designed to force freed blacks to work on plantations, where they would be put to work in gangs. These codes denied blacks the right to purchase or even rent land. Vagrancy laws allowed authorities to arrest blacks "in idleness" and assign them to a chain gang or auction them off to a planter for as long as a year. Other statutes required blacks to have written proof of employment and barred blacks from leaving plantations. The Freedmen's Bureau, ostensibly designed to aid former slaves, helped to enforce laws against vagrancy and loitering and refused to allow ex-slaves to keep land that they had occupied during the war. One black army veteran asked rhetorically: "If you call this Freedom, what did you call Slavery?"

Such efforts to virtually reenslave the freedmen led Congressional Republicans to seize control of Reconstruction from President Andrew Johnson, deny representatives from the former Confederate states their Congressional seats, and pass the Civil Rights Act of 1866 and write the Fourteenth Amendment to the Constitution, extending citizenship rights to African-Americans and guaranteeing them equal protection of the laws. In 1870, the country went even further by ratifying the Fifteenth Amendment, which gave voting rights to black men. The most radical proposal advanced during Reconstruction—to confiscate plantations and redistribute portions of the land to the freedmen—was defeated.

The freedmen, in alliance with carpetbaggers (northerners who had migrated to the South following the Civil War) and southern white Republicans known as scalawags, temporarily gained power in every former Confederate state except Virginia. Altogether, over 600 blacks served as legislators in Reconstruction governments (though blacks comprised the majority of legislators only in the lower house of South Carolina's legislature). The Reconstruction governments drew up democratic state constitutions, expanded women's rights, provided debt relief, and established the South's first state-funded schools. During the 1870s, however, internal divisions within the southern Republican party, white terror, and northern apathy allowed white Democrats, known as Redeemers, to return to power in the South's state governments. The North's failure to enforce the 14th and 15th Amendments, permitted racial segregation and disfranchisement in the South.

During Reconstruction, former slaves—and many small white farmers—became trapped in a new system of economic exploitation known as sharecropping. Lacking capital and land of their own, former slaves were forced to work for large landowners. Initially, planters, with the support of the Freedmen's Bureau, sought to restore gang labor under the supervision of white overseers. But the freedman, who wanted autonomy and independence, refused to sign contracts that required gang labor. Ultimately, sharecropping emerged as a sort of compromise.

Instead of cultivating land in gangs supervised by overseers, landowners divided plantations into 20- to 50-acre plots suitable for farming by a single family. In exchange for land, a cabin, and supplies, sharecroppers agreed to raise a cash crop (usually cotton) and to give half the crop to their landlord. The high interest rates landlords and merchants charged for goods bought on credit transformed sharecropping into a system of economic dependency and poverty. The freedmen found that "freedom could make folks proud but it didn't make 'em rich."

Nevertheless, the sharecropping system did allow freedmen a degree of freedom and autonomy greater than that experienced under slavery. As a symbol of their newly won independence, freedmen had teams of mules drag their former slave cabins away from the slave quarters into their own fields. Black wives and daughters sharply reduced their labor in the fields and instead devoted more time to childcare and housework. For the first time, black families could divide their time between fieldwork and housework in accordance with their own family priorities.

Chattel slavery had been defeated. The gang system of labor, enforced by the whip, was dead. Real gains had been won though full freedom remained an unfulfilled promise.

*   *   *

In 1970, the countries of the Arabian peninsula became the last in the world to abolish legal slavery. Nevertheless, the buying and selling of human beings continues to flourish in many parts of the world. Each year, an estimated one million Asian women and children, in Bangladesh, Burma, India, Pakistan, Sri Lanka, Thailand, and elsewhere, are sold or auctioned into slavery to serve as prostitutes or child laborers. Methods of procurement have changed since the eighteenth century; instead of being kidnapped, slaves are bought from impoverished village leaders for a few hundred dollars. So the cruelties of slavery remain, with contemporary slaves chained to beds in brothels or at workbenches in sweatshops. The final chapter in the history of slavery cannot yet be written.

Part 1

ENSLAVEMENT:

"Death's Gwineter Lay His Cold Icy Hands on Me"

In 1441, a Portuguese sailor named Antam Concalvez sailed south to what is now Morocco, carrying a cargo of sea lion skins and oil. During the voyage, Concalvez reportedly expressed a desire to please Prince Henry of Portugal by bringing him African captives. While ashore, his crew wounded an African with a javelin and took him prisoner and subsequently captured an African woman. Then the crew staged a raid, in which four Africans were killed and ten others were captured. The capture of these twelve African prisoners marked the beginning of the European slave trade with sub-Saharan Africa.

The best estimates of Africans caught in the Atlantic slave trade over the next four centuries suggest that over nine-and-a-half million Africans were forcibly imported into the New World and that another two million died during the Middle Passage. But no one knows how many people died in Africa during wars in which slaves were seized, in the forced march to the coast, or in the coastal dungeons, pens, and "barracoons," where slaves were herded. This figure may well have been more than seven million, bringing the total number of Africans entrapped in the slave trade to more than eighteen million people.

As early as the mid-1450s, Europeans began to acquire West African slaves through trade rather than raids. By the seventeenth century, the English, French, Dutch, Danes, and Swedes had joined the Portuguese and Spanish in the African slave trade. Along the West African coast, European merchants established forts and trading posts—known as "factories" or "castles"—to serve as centers for collecting slaves.

Within West Africa, war, crop failure, drought, famine, political instability, small-scale raiding, taxation, and judicial or religious

29

punishment generated large number of slaves. War captives, condemned criminals, debtors, aliens, famine victims, and political dissidents—all might find themselves sold into slavery.

The slave trade was greatly abetted by the low cost of slaves. Even though the price of slaves rose three- or four-fold during the eighteenth century, many Europeans were convinced that it was "cheaper to buy than to breed." Between the sixteenth and mideighteenth centuries, it was cheaper to import a slave from Africa than to raise a child to the age of fourteen. During the late seventeenth century, merchants in the Senegambia region of West Africa paid as little as one pound sterling for a young male, whom they sold to Europeans traders for the equivalent of three-and-a-half pounds sterling, or 11 muskets, 31 gallons of brandy, or 93 pounds of wrought iron. Initially, many slaves were acquired from regions within fifty or one hundred miles of the West African coast. During the eighteenth century, however, rising prices led slavers to search for captives in interior regions, 500 to 1,000 miles inland.

The impact of the slave trade on West African society is almost impossible to calculate. The demographic consequences are the most obvious. While the slave trade probably did not drastically depopulate West Africa, it may well have caused sharp population declines in particular regions and it certainly kept the overall population growth rate low.

The slave trade had other high social costs as well. Throughout West Africa, the slave trade fostered warfare, skewed local economies, expanded servitude within the region, and distorted class and political structures. While the slave trade enhanced the power, prestige, and wealth of particular West African rulers, merchants, and states, it contributed to economic stagnation and long-term political instability. The introduction of European guns and gunpowder reinforced political fragmentation, allowing particular states to grow at the expense of other states. Meanwhile, the influx of European textiles and manufactured goods undermined local West African industries.

Of course, the greatest cost of the slave trade was its human toll. The selections that follow document the African side of the Atlantic slave trade: capture, transit to the coast, and sale to Europeans. They disclose the human meaning of enslavement as told by those who would know best, its victims.

1
John Barbot

"PREPOSSESSED OF THE OPINION . . . THAT EUROPEANS ARE FOND OF THEIR FLESH"

John Barbot, an agent for the French Royal African Company, made at least two voyages to the West Coast of Africa, in 1678 and 1682.

Those sold by the Blacks are for the most part prisoners of war, taken either in fight, or pursuit, or in the incursions they make into their enemies' territories; others stolen away by their own countrymen; and some there are, who will sell their own children, kindred, or neighbours. This has been often seen, and to compass it, they desire the person they intend to sell, to help them in carrying something to the factory by way of trade, and when there, the person so deluded, not understanding the language, is sold and deliver'd up as a slave, notwithstanding all his resistance, and exclaiming against the treachery. . . .

The kings are so absolute, that upon any slight pretense of offences committed by their subjects, they order them to be sold for slaves, without regard to rank, or possession. . . .

Abundance of little Blacks of both sexes are also stolen away by their neighbours, when found abroad on the roads, or in the woods; or else in the Cougans, or corn-fields, at the time of the year, when their parents keep them there all day, to scare away the devouring small birds, that come to feed on the millet, in swarms, as has been said above.

In times of dearth and famine, abundance of those people will sell themselves, for a maintenance, and to prevent starving. When I first arriv'd at Goerree, in December, 1681, I could have bought a

---

Source: John Barbot, "A Description of the Coasts of North and South Guinea," in Thomas Astley and John Churchill, eds., *Collection of Voyages and Travels* (London, 1732).

great number, at very easy rates, if I could have found provisions to subsist them; so great was the dearth then, in that part of Nigritia.

To conclude, some slaves are also brought to these Blacks, from very remote inland countries, by way of trade, and sold for things of very inconsiderable value; but these slaves are generally poor and weak, by reason of the barbarous usage they have had in traveling so far, being continually beaten, and almost famish'd; so inhuman are the Blacks to one another. . . .

The trade of slaves is in a more peculiar manner the business of kings, rich men, and prime merchants, exclusive of the inferior sort of Blacks.

These slaves are severely and barbarously treated by their masters, who subsist them poorly, and beat them inhumanly, as may be seen by the scabs and wounds on the bodies of many of them when sold to us. They scarce allow them the least rag to cover their nakedness, which they also take off from them when sold to Europeans; and they always go bare-headed. The wives and children of slaves, are also slaves to the master under whom they are married; and when dead, they never bury them, but cast out the bodies into some by place, to be devoured by birds, or beasts of prey.

This barbarous usage of those unfortunate wretches, makes it appear, that the fate of such as are bought and transported from the coast to America, or other parts of the world, by Europeans, is less deplorable, than that of those who end their days in their native country; for aboard ships all possible care is taken to preserve and subsist them for the interest of the owners, and when sold in America, the same motive ought to prevail with their masters to use them well, that they may live the longer, and do them more service. Not to mention the inestimable advantage they may reap, of becoming Christians, and saving their souls, if they make a true use of their condition. . . .

Many of those slaves we transport from Guinea to America are prepossessed with the opinion, that they are carried like sheep to the slaughter, and that the Europeans are fond of their flesh; which notion so far prevails with some, as to make them fall into a deep melancholy and despair, and to refuse all sustenance, tho' never so much compelled and even beaten to oblige them to take some nourishment: notwithstanding all which, they will starve to death; whereof I have had several instances in my own slaves both aboard and at Guadalupe. And tho' I must say I am naturally compassionate, yet have I been necessitated sometimes to cause the teeth of those wretches to be broken, because they would not open their mouths, or be prevailed upon by any entreaties to feed themselves; and thus have forced some sustenance into their throats. . . .

As the slaves come down to Fida from the inland country, they are put into a booth, or prison, built for that purpose, near the beach, all of them together; and when the Europeans are to receive them, every part of every one of them, to the smallest member, men and women being all stark naked. Such as are allowed good and sound, are set on one side, and the others by themselves; which slaves so rejected are there called Mackrons, being above thirty-five years of age, or defective in their limbs, eyes or teeth; or grown grey, or that have the venereal disease, or any other imperfection. These being set aside, each of the others, which have passed as good, is marked on the breast, with a red-hot iron, imprinting the mark of the French, English, or Dutch companies, that so each nation may distinguish their own, and to prevent their being chang'd by the natives for worse, as they are apt enough to do. In this particular, care is taken that the women, as tenderest, be not burnt too hard.

The branded slaves, after this, are returned to their former booth, where the factor is to subsist them at his own charge, which amounts to about two-pence a day for each of them, with bread and water, which is all their allowance. There they continue sometimes ten or fifteen days, till the sea is still enough to send them aboard; for very often it continues too boisterous for so long a time, unless in January, February and March, which is commonly the calmest season: and when it is so, the slaves are carried off by parcels, in bar-canoes, and put aboard the ships in the road. Before they enter the canoes, or come out of the booth, their former Black masters strip them of every rag they have, without distinction of men or women; to supply which, in orderly ships, each of them as they come aboard is allowed a piece of canvas, to wrap around their waist, which is very acceptable to those poor wretches. . . .

If there happens to be no stock of slaves at Fida, the factor must trust the Blacks with his goods, to the value of a hundred and fifty, or two hundred slaves; which goods they carry up into the inland, to buy slaves, at all the markets, for above two hundred leagues up the country, where they are kept like cattle in Europe; the slaves sold there being generally prisoners of war, taken from their enemies, like other booty, and perhaps some few sold by their own countrymen, in extreme want, or upon a famine; as also some as a punishment of heinous crimes: tho' many Europeans believe that parents sell their own children, men their wives and relations, which, if it ever happens, is so seldom, that it cannot justly be charged upon a whole nation, as a custom and common practice. . . .

One thing is to be taken notice of by sea-faring men, that this Fida and Ardra slaves are of all the others, the most apt to revolt aboard ships, by a conspiracy carried on amongst themselves; especially such as are brought down to Fida, from very remote inland countries, who easily draw others into their plot: for being used to see men's flesh eaten in their own country, and publick markets held for the purpose, they are very full of the notion, that we buy and transport them to the same purpose; and will therefore watch all opportunities to deliver themselves, by assaulting a ship's crew, and murdering them all, if possible: whereof, we have almost every year some instances, in one European ship or other, that is filled with slaves.

2
Ayubah Suleiman Diallo

"HE WAS NO COMMON SLAVE"

Any West African, regardless of status, might be enslaved. Ayubah Suleiman Diallo, who was born around 1701 to a family of Muslim clerics, was a well-educated merchant in the Senegambian region of West Africa, which had supplied Europe with beeswax, gold, gum, ivory, and small numbers of slaves since the fifteenth century. In 1730, he was kidnapped and transported to Maryland. From here he wrote a letter to his father, which came to the attention of James Oglethorpe, the founder of Georgia, who helped purchase his freedom and bring him to England, where he was known as Job ben Solomon.

In February, 1730, Job's father hearing of an English ship at Gambia River, sent him, with two servants to attend him, to sell two Negroes, and to buy paper, and other necessities; but desired him not to venture over the river, because the country of the Mandingoes, who are enemies . . . lies on the other side. Job not agreeing with Captain Pike . . . sent back the two servants to acquaint his father with it, and to let him know that he intended to go farther. Accordingly having agreed with another man, named Loumein Yoas, who understood the Mandingoe language, to go with him as his interpreter, he crossed the River Gambia, and disposed of his Negroes for some cows. As he was returning home, he stopped for some refreshment at the house of an old acquaintance; and the weather being hot, he hung up his arms in the house, while he refreshed himself. Those arms were very valuable; consisting of a gold-hilted sword, a gold knife, which they wear by their side, and a rich quiver of arrows, which King Sambo had made him a pres-

Source: Thomas Bluett, *Some Memoirs of the Life of Job, the Son of Solomon* (London, 1734).

ent of. It happened that a company of the Mandingoes, who live upon plunder, passing by at that time, and observing him unarmed, rushed in, to the number of seven or eight at once, at a back door, and pinioned Job, before he could get to his arms, together with his interpreter, who is a slave in Maryland still. They then shaved their heads and beards, which Job and his man resented as the highest indignity; tho' the Mandingoes meant no more by it, than to make them appear like Slaves taken in war. On the 27th of February, 1730, they carried them to Captain Pike at Gambia, who purchased them; and on the first of March they were put on board. Soon after Job found means to acquaint Captain Pike that he was the same person that came to trade with him a few days before, and after what manner he had been taken. Upon this Captain Pike gave him leave to redeem himself and his man; and Job sent to an acquaintance of his father's, near Gambia, who promised to send to Job's father, to inform him of what had happened, that he might take some course to have him set at liberty. But it being a fortnight's journey between that friend's house and his father's, and the ship sailing in about a week after, Job was brought with the rest of the slaves to Annapolis and Maryland, and delivered to Mr. Vachell Denton, factor to Mr. Hunt, before mentioned. Job heard since, by vessels that came from Gambia, that his father sent down several slaves, a little after Captain Pike sailed, in order to procure his redemption; and that Sambo, King of Futa, had made war upon the Mandingoes, and cut off great numbers of them, upon of the account of the injury they had done to his schoolfellow.

Mr. Vachell Denton sold Job to one Mr. Tolsey in Kent Island in Maryland, who put him to work in making tobacco; but he was soon convinced that Job had never been used to such labour. He every day showed more and more uneasiness under this exercise, and at last grew sick, being no way able to bear it; so that his master was obliged to find easier work for him, and therefore put him to tend the cattle. Job would often leave the cattle, and withdraw into the woods to pray; but a white boy frequently watched him, and whilst he was at his devotion would mock him, and throw dirt in his face. This very much disturbed Job, and added considerably to his other misfortunes; all which were increased by his ignorance of the English language, which prevented him from complaining, or telling his case to any person about him. Grown in some measure desperate, by reason of his present hardship, he resolved to travel at a venture; thinking he might possibly be taken up by some master, who would use him better or otherwise meet with some lucky accident, to divert or abate his grief. Accordingly, he travelled thro' the woods, till he came to the County of Kent, upon Delaware Bay, now esteemed part of Pensilvania; altho' it is properly a part of Maryland, and belongs to my Lord Baltimore. There is a law in force, throughout the colonies of Virginia, Maryland, Pensilvania, etc. as far as Boston in New England, viz. that any Negroe, or white servant who is not known in the county, or has no pass, may be secured by any person, and kept in the common gaol, till the master of such servant shall fetch him. Therefore Job being able to give no account of himself, was put in prison there.

This happened about the beginning of June, 1731 when I, who was attending the courts there, and had heard of Job, went with several gentlemen to the gaoler's house, being a tavern, and desired to see him. He was brought into the tavern to us, but could not speak one word of English. Upon our taking and making signs to him, he wrote a line or two before us, and when he read it, pronounced the words Allah and Mahommed; by which, and his refusing a glass of wine we offered him, we perceived he was a Mahomedtan, but could not imagine of what country he was, or how he got thither; for by his affable carriage, and the easy composure of his countenance, we could perceive he was no common slave.

When Job had been some time confined, an old Negroe man, who lived in that neighbourhood, and could speak the Jalloff language, which Job also understood, went to him, and conversed with him. By this Negroe the keeper was informed to whom Job belonged, and what was the cause of his leaving his master. The keeper thereupon wrote to his master, who soon after fetched him home, and was much kinder to him than before; allowing him a place to pray in, and some other conveniences, in order to make his slavery as easy as possible. Yet slavery and confinement was by no means agreeable to Job, who had never been used to it; he therefore wrote a letter in Arabick to his father, acquainting him with his misfortunes, hoping he might yet find means to redeem him. This letter he sent to Mr. Vachell Denton, desiring it might be sent to Africa by Captain Pike; but he being gone to England, Mr. Denton sent the letter inclosed to Mr. Hunt, in order to be sent to Africa by Captain Pike from England; but Captain Pike had sailed for Africa before the letter came to Mr. Hunt, who therefore kept it in his own hands, till he should have a proper opportunity of sending it. It happened that this letter was seen by James Oglethorpe, Esq. [an English philanthropist who founded the colony of Georgia as a haven for debtors], who, according to his usual goodness and generosity, took compassion on Job, and gave his bond to Mr. Hunt for the payment of a certain sum, upon the delivery of Job here in England. Mr. Hunt upon this sent to Mr. Denton, who purchased him again of his master for the same money which Mr. Denton had formerly received for him; his master being very willing to part with him, as finding him no ways fit for his business.

3
Olaudah Equiano

"THEY . . . CARRY OFF
AS MANY AS THEY CAN SEIZE"

Olaudah Equiano, an Ibo from Nigeria, was just eleven years old when he was kidnapped into slavery. He was held captive in West Africa for seven months and then sold to British slavers, who shipped him to Barbados and then took him to Virginia. After serving a British naval officer, he was sold to a Quaker merchant from Philadelphia who allowed him to purchase his freedom in 1766. In later life, he played an active role in the movement to abolish the slave trade.

My father, besides many slaves, had a numerous family, of which seven lived to grow up, including myself and a sister, who was the only daughter. As I was the youngest of the sons, I became, of course, the greatest favourite of my mother, and was always with her; and she used to take particular pains to form my mind. I was trained up from my earliest years in the arts of agriculture and war; and my mother adorned me with emblems, after the manner of our greatest warriors. In this way I grew up till I was turned the age of eleven, when an end was put to my happiness in the following manner:—Generally, when the grown people in the neighbourhood were gone far in the fields to labour, the children assembled together in some of the neighborhood's premises to play; and commonly some of us used to get up a tree to look out for any assailant, or kidnapper, that might come upon us; for they sometimes took those opportunities of our parents' absence, to attack and carry off as many as they could seize. One day, as I was watching at the top of a tree in our yard, I saw one of those people come into the yard

Source: *The Interesting Narrative of the Life of Olaudah Equiano or Gustavus Vassa the African* (London, 1789).

of our next neighbour but one, to kidnap, there being many stout young people in it. Immediately, on this, I gave the alarm of the rogue, and he was surrounded by the stoutest of them, who entangled him with cords, so that he could not escape till some of the grown people came and secured him. But alas! ere long, it was my fate to be thus attacked, and to be carried off, when none of the grown people were nigh. One day, when all our people were gone out to their works as usual, and only I and my dear sister were left to mind the house, two men and a woman got over our walls, and in a moment seized us both; and, without giving us time to cry out, or make resistance, they stopped our mouths, and ran off with us into the nearest wood. Here they tied our hands, and continued to carry us as far as they could, till night came on, when we reached a small house, where the robbers halted for refreshment, and spent the night. We were then unbound; but were unable to take any food; and, being quite overpowered by fatigue and grief, our only relief was some sleep, which allayed our misfortune for a short time.

4
Venture Smith

"I THEN HAD A ROPE PUT ABOUT MY NECK"

Kidnapped at the age of six, Venture Smith was sold to the steward on a slave ship and brought to Connecticut. At the age of thirty-one, after several changes of ownership, he purchased his freedom with money that he earned by hiring out his labor and "cleaning musk-rats and minks, raising potatoes and carrots, and by fishing in the night, and at odd spells." In order to purchase his wife and sons, he fished, sailed on a whaler, ferried wood from Long Island to Rhode Island, and raised watermelons. Later, he actually became a slaveholder, purchasing at least three slaves. At his death at the age of seventy-seven in 1805 in East Haddam, Connecticut, he left a hundred-acre farm and three houses.

I was born in Dukandarra, in Guinea, about the year 1729. My father's name was Saungm Furro, Prince of the tribe of Dukandarra. My father had three wives. Polygamy was not uncommon in that country, especially among the rich, as every man was allowed to keep as many wives as he could maintain. . . .

The first thing worthy of notice which I remember was, a contention between my father and mother, on account of my father marrying his third wife without the consent of his first and eldest, which was contrary to the custom generally observed among my countrymen. In consequence of this rupture, my mother left her husband and country, and travelled away with her three children to the eastward. I was then five years old. . . . After five days travel . . . my mother was pleased to stop and seek a refuge for me. She left me at the house of a very rich farmer. I was then, as I should

Source: *A Narrative of the Life and Adventures of Venture, A Native of Africa* (New London, Conn., 1798; expanded ed., Hamden, Conn., 1896).

judge, not less than one hundred and forty miles from my native place, separated from all my relations and acquaintance....

My father sent a man and horse after me. After settling with my guardian for keeping me, he took me away and went for home. It was then about one year since my mother brought me here. Nothing remarkable occurred to us on our journey until we arrived safe home.

I found then that the difference between my parents had been made up previous to their sending for me. On my return, I was received both by my father and mother with great joy and affection, and was once more restored to my paternal dwelling in peace and happiness. I was then about six years old.

Not more than six weeks had passed after my return before a message was brought by an inhabitant of the place where I lived the preceding year to my father, that that place had been invaded by a numerous army from a nation not far distant, furnished with musical instrument, and all kinds of arms then in use; that they were instigated by some white nation who equipped and sent them to subdue and possess the country; that his nation had made no preparation for war, having been for a long time in profound peace; that they could not defend themselves against such a formidable train of invaders, and must therefore necessarily evacuate their lands to the fierce enemy, and fly to the protection of some chief; and that if he would permit them they would come under his rule and protection when they had to retreat from their own possessions. He was a kind and merciful prince, and therefore consented to these proposals....

He gave them every privilege and all the protection his government could afford. But they had not been there longer than four days before news came to them that the invaders had laid waste their country, and were coming speedily to destroy them in my father's territories. This affrighted them, and therefore they immediately pushed off to the southward, into the unknown countries there, and were never more heard of.

Two days after their retreat, the report turned out to be but too true. A detachment from the enemy came to my father and informed him, that the whole army was encamped not far out of his dominions, and would invade the territory and deprive his people of their liberties and rights, if he did not comply with the following terms. These were to pay them a large sum of money, three hundred fat cattle, and a great number of goats, sheep, asses, etc.

My father told the messenger he would comply rather than that his subjects should be deprived of their rights and privileges, which he was not then in circumstances to defend from so sudden an invasion. Upon turning out those articles, the enemy pledged their faith and honor that they would not attack him. On these he relied and therefore thought it unnecessary to be on his guard against the enemy. But their pledges of faith and honor proved no better than those of other unprincipled hostile nations; for a few days after a certain relation of the king came and informed him, that the enemy who sent terms of accommodation to him and received tribute to their satisfaction, yet meditated an attack upon his subjects by surprise and that probably they would commence their attack in less than one day, and concluded with advising him, as he was not prepared for war, to order a speedy retreat of his family and subjects. He complied with this advice.

The same night which was fixed upon to retreat, my father and his family set off about the break of day. The king and his two younger wives went in one company, and my mother and her children in another. We left our dwellings in succession, and my father's company went on first. We directed our course for a large shrub plain, some distance off, where we intended to conceal ourselves from the approaching enemy, until we could refresh ourselves a little. But we presently found that our retreat was not secure. For having struck up a little fire for the purpose of cooking victuals, the enemy who happened to be encamped a little distance off, had sent out a scouting party who discovered us by the smoke of the fire, just as we were extinguishing it, and about to eat. As soon as we had finished eating, my father discovered the party, and immediately began to discharge arrows at them. This was what I first saw, and it alarmed both me and the women, who being unable to make any resistance, immediately betook ourselves to the tall thick reeds not far off, and left the old king to fight alone. For some time I beheld him from the reeds defending himself with great courage and firmness, till at last he was obliged to surrender himself into their hands.

They then came to us in the reeds, and the very first salute I had from them was a violent blow on the back part of the head with the fore part of a gun, and at the same time a grasp round the neck. I then had a rope put about my neck, as had all the women in the thicket with me, and were immediately led to my father, who was likewise pinioned and haltered for leading. In this condition we were all led to the camp. The women and myself being pretty submissive, had tolerable treatment from the enemy, while my father was closely interrogated respecting his money which they knew he must have. But as he gave them no account of it, he was instantly cut and pounded on his body with great inhumanity, that he might be induced by the torture he suffered to make the discovery. All this availed not in the least to make him give up his money, but he despised all the tortures which they inflicted, until the continued exercise and increase of torment, obliged him to sink and expire. He thus died without informing his enemies where his money lay. I saw him while he was thus tortured to death. The shocking scene is to this day fresh in my mind, and I have often been overcome while thinking on it. . . .

The army of the enemy was large, I should suppose consisting of about six thousand men. Their leader was called Baukurre. After destroying the old prince, they decamped and immediately marched toward the sea, lying to the West, taking with them myself and the women prisoners. In the march a scouting party was detached from the main army. To the leader of this party I was made waiter, having to carry his gun, etc. As we were a scouting we came across a herd of fat cattle, consisting of about thirty in number. These we set upon, and immediately wrested from their keepers, and afterwards converted them into food for the army. The enemy had remarkable success in destroying the country wherever they went. For as far as they had penetrated, they laid the habitations waste and captured the people. The distance they had now brought me was about four hundred miles. All the march I had very hard tasks imposed on me, which I must perform on pain of punishment. I was obliged to carry on my head a large glat stone used for grinding our corn, weighing as I should suppose, as much as twenty-five pounds; besides victuals, mat and cooking utensils. Though I was pretty large and stout at my age, yet these burdens were very grievous to me, being only six years and a half old.

We were then come to a place called Malagasco. When we entered the place we could not see the least appearance of either houses or inhabitants, but upon stricter search found, that instead of houses above ground they had dens in the sides of hillocks, contiguous to ponds and streams of water. In these we perceived they had all hid themselves, as I supposed they usually did on such occas..ons. In order to compel them to surrender, the enemy contrived to smoke them out with faggots. These they put to the entrance of the caves and set them on fire. While they were engaged in this business, to their great surprise some of them were desperately wounded with arrows which fell from above on them. This mystery they soon found out. They perceived that the enemy discharged these arrows through holes on top of the dens, directly into the air. Their weight brought them back, point downwards on their enemies heads, whilst they were smoking the inhabitants out. The points of their arrows were poisoned, but their enemy had an antidote for it, which they instantly applied to the wounded part. The smoke at last obliged the people to give themselves up. They came out of their caves, first putting the palms of their hands together, and immediately after extended their arms, crossed at their wrists, ready to be bound and pinioned. . . .

The invaders then pinioned the prisoners of all ages and sexes indiscriminately, took their flocks and all their effects, and moved on their way towards the sea. On the march the prisoners were treated with clemency, on account of their being submissive and humble. Having come to the next tribe, the enemy laid siege and immediately took men, women, children, flocks, and all their valuable effects. They then went on to the next district which was contiguous to the sea, called in Africa, Anamaboo. The enemies' provisions were then almost spent, as well as their strength. The inhabitants knowing what conduct they had pursued, and what were their present intentions, improved the favorable opportunity, attacked them, and took enemy, prisoners, flocks and all their effects. I was then taken a second time. All of us were then put into the castle [a European slave trading post], and kept for market. On a certain time I and other prisoners were put on board a canoe, under our master, and rowed away to a vessel belonging to Rhode Island, commanded by Captain Collingwood, and the mate Thomas Mumford. While we were going to the vessel, our master told us all to appear to the best possible advantage for sale. I was bought on board by one Robert Mumford, steward of said vessel, for four gallons of rum, and a piece of calico, and called Venture, on account of his having purchased me with his own private venture. Thus I came by my name. All the slaves that were bought for that vessel's cargo, were two hundred and sixty.

Part 2

THE MIDDLE PASSAGE:

"God's A-Gwineter Trouble de Water"

When the British frigate North Star *stopped and boarded a slave ship in the South Atlantic in 1829—two decades after the United States and Britain outlawed the Atlantic slave trade—the crew found conditions aboard the slaver almost unspeakably horrible. Its cargo consisted of 505 African men and women. Another 55 had been tossed overboard during 17 days at sea. The slaves "were all enclosed under grated hatchways, between decks. The space was so low that they sat between each others' legs, and stowed so close together, that there was no possibility of lying down, or at all changing their position, by night or by day. . . . They were all branded like sheep . . . burnt with a red hot iron. . . . " Each captive, chained by the neck and legs, had just one square foot of sitting space.*

No aspect of the Atlantic slave trade aroused more passionate denunciation than the Middle Passage—the transoceanic voyage to the New World. On many ships, slaves were crowded almost beyond belief. Typically, slaves had less than half the space provided for convicts aboard prison ships. A parliamentary inquiry concluded that conditions aboard the British slaver Brookes *were fairly typical. To carry its cargo of 451 slaves, every man was allowed a space just 6' long, 16" wide, and 2' 7" high; every woman, a space 5' 10" long and 16" wide; every boy, 5' by 14"; every girl, 4' 6" by 12". But on at least one voyage, the ship carried as many as 609 slaves.*

Average death rates were extraordinary, running as high as 168 deaths for every 1,000 slaves leaving the African coast. Average child mortality was even higher. Some voyages were particularly deadly. The British slaver Hero *lost 360 slaves—over half its slaves—mainly from smallpox; the* Briton *lost half its 375 slaves.*

The major cause of death was ameobic dysentery—"the bloody flux"— caused by contaminated food and water supplies, reflecting the low level of sanitation aboard the ships. Other killers included small pox, measles, and other communicable diseases. In addition, many slaves died in shipboard revolts, attacks by pirates, and shipwrecks—or from suicide.

5
James Barbot, Jr.

"PREMEDITATED A REVOLT"

James Barbot, Jr., a sailor aboard the English slaver Don Carlos, *describes a slave uprising that took place aboard the vessel.*

About one in the afternoon, after dinner, we, according to custom caused them, one by one, to go down between decks, to have each his pint of water; most of them were yet above deck, many of them provided with knives, which we had indiscreetly given them two or three days before, as not suspecting the least attempt of this nature from them; others had pieces of iron they had torn off our forecastle door, as having premeditated a revolt, and seeing all the ship's company, at best but weak and many quite sick, they had also broken off the shackles from several of their companions' feet, which served them, as well as billets they had provided themselves with, and all other things they could lay hands on, which they imagin'd might be of use for this enterprize. Thus arm'd, they fell in crouds and parcels on our men, upon the deck unawares, and stabb'd one of the stoutest of us all, who receiv'd fourteen or fifteen wounds of their knives, and so expir'd. Next they assaulted our boatswain, and cut one of his legs so round the bone, that he could not move, the nerves being cut through; others cut our cook's throat to the pipe, and others wounded three of the sailors, and threw one of them over-board in that condition, from the forecastle into the sea; who, however, by good providence, got hold of the bowline of the fore-sail, and sav'd himself . . . we stood in arms, firing on the revolted slaves, of whom we kill'd some, and wounded many: which so terrif'd the rest, that they gave way, dispersing

---

Source: James Barbot, Jr., "A Supplement to the Description of the Coasts of North and South Guinea," in Awnsham and John Churchill, *Collection of Voyages and Travels* (London, 1732).

themselves some one way and some another between decks, and under the fore-castle; and many of the most mutinous, leapt over board, and drown'd themselves in the ocean with much resolution, shewing no manner of concern for life. Thus we lost twenty seven or twenty eight slaves, either kill'd by us, or drown'd; and having master'd them, caused all to go betwixt decks, giving them good words. The next day we had them all again upon deck, where they unanimously declar'd, the Menbombe slaves had been the contrivers of the mutiny, and for an example we caused about thirty of the ringleaders to be very severely whipt by all our men that were capable of doing that office. . . .

I have observ'd, that the great mortality, which so often happens in slave-ships, proceeds as well from taking in too many, as from want of knowing how to manage them aboard. . . .

As to the management of our slaves aboard, we lodge the two sexes apart, by means of a strong partition at the main mast; the forepart is for men, the other behind the mast for the women. If it be in large ships carrying five or six hundred slaves, the deck in such ships ought to be at least five and a half or six foot high, which is very requisite for driving a continual trade of slaves: for the greater height it has, the more airy and convenient it is for such a considerable number of human creatures; and consequently far the more healthy for them, and fitter to look after them. We build a sort of half-deck along the sides with deals and spars provided for that purpose in Europe, that half-deck extending no farther than the sides of our scuttles and so the slaves lie in two rows, one above the other, and as close together as they can be crouded. . . .

The planks, or deals, contract some dampness more or less, either from the deck being so often wash'd to keep it clean and sweet, or from the rain that gets in now and then through the scuttles or other openings, and even from the very sweat of the slaves; which being so crouded in a low place, is perpetual, and occasions many distempers, or at best great inconveniences dangerous to their health. . . .

It has been observ'd before, that some slaves fancy they are carry'd to be eaten, which make them desperate; and others are so on account of their captivity: so that if care be not taken, they will mutiny and destroy the ship's crue in hopes to get away.

To prevent such misfortunes, we used to visit them daily, narrowly searching every corner between decks, to see whether they have not found means, to gather any pieces of iron, or wood, or knives, about the ship, notwithstanding the great care we take not to leave any tools or nails, or other things in the way: which, however, cannot be always so exactly observ'd, where so many people are in the narrow compass of a ship.

We cause as many of our men as is convenient to lie in the quarter-deck and gun-room, and our principal officers in the great cabin, where we keep all our small arms in a readiness, with sentinels constantly at the doors and avenues to it; being thus ready to disappoint any attempts our slave might make on a sudden.

These precautions contribute very much to keep them in awe; and if all those who carry slaves duly observ'd them, we should not hear of so many revolts as have happen'd. Where I was concern'd, we always kept our slaves in such order, that we did not perceive the least inclination in any of them to revolt, or mutiny, and lost very few of our number in the voyage.

It is true, we allow'd them much more liberty, and us'd them with more tenderness than most other Europeans would think prudent to do; as, to have them all upon deck every day in good weather; to take their meals twice a-day, at fix'd hours, that is, at ten in the morning, and at five at night; which being ended, we made the men go down again between the decks; for the women were almost entirely at their own discretion, to be upon deck as long as they pleas'd, nay even many of the males had the same liberty by turns, successively; few or none being fetter'd or kept in shackles, and that only on account of some disturbances, or injuries, offer'd to their fellow captives, as will unavoidably happen among a numerous croud of such savage people. Besides, we allow'd each of them betwixt their meals a handful of Indian wheat and Mandioca, and now and then short pipes and tobacco to smoak upon deck by turns, and some coconuts; and to the women a piece of coarse cloth to cover them, and the same to many of the men, which we took care they did wash from time to time, to prevent vermin, which they are very subject to; and because it look'd sweeter and more agreeable. Toward the evening they diverted themselves on the deck, as they thought fit, some conversing together, others dancing, singing, and sporting after their manner, which pleased them highly, and often made us pastime; especially the female sex, who being apart from the males, on the quarter-deck, and many of them young sprightly maidens, full of jollity and good-humour, afforded us abundance of recreation; as did several little fine boys, which we mostly kept to attend on us about the ship.

We mess'd the slaves twice a day, as I have observed; the first meal was of our large beans boil'd, with a certain quantity of Muscovy lard. . . . The other meal was of pease, or of Indian wheat, and sometimes meal of Mandioca . . . boiled with either lard, or suet, or grease by turns: and sometimes with palm-oil and malaguette or Guinea pepper I found they had much better stomachs for beans, and it is a proper fattening food for captives. . . .

At each meal we allow'd every slave a full coconut shell of water, and from time to time a dram of brandy, to strengthen their stomachs. . . .

Much more might be said relating to the preservation and maintenance of slaves in such voyages, which I leave to the prudence of the officers that govern aboard, if they value their own reputation and their owners' advantage; and shall only add these few particulars, that tho' we ought to be circumspect in watching the slaves narrowly, to prevent or disappoint their ill designs for our own conservation, yet must we not be too severe and haughty with them, but on the contrary, caress and humor them in every reasonable thing. Some commanders, of a morose peevish temper are perpetually beating and curbing them, even without the least offence, and will not suffer any upon deck but when unavoidable to ease themselves does require; under pretence it hinders the work of the ship and sailors and that they are troublesome by their nasty nauseous stench, or their noise; which makes those poor wretches desperate, and besides their falling into distempers thro' melancholy, often is the occasion of their destroying themselves.

Such officers should consider, those unfortunate creatures are men as well as themselves, tho' of a different colour, and pagans; and that they ought to do to others as they would be done by in like circumstances. . . .

6
Olaudah Equiano

"A MULTITUDE OF
BLACK PEOPLE . . . CHAINED TOGETHER"

Olaudah Equiano vividly recounts the shock and isolation that he felt during the Middle Passage to Barbados and his fear that the European slavers would eat him.

Their complexions, differing so much from ours, their long hair and the language they spoke, which was different from any I had ever heard, united to confirm me in this belief. Indeed, such were the horrors of my views and fears at the moment, that if ten thousand worlds had been my own, I would have freely parted with them all to have exchanged my condition with that of the meanest slave of my own country. When I looked around the ship and saw a large furnace of copper boiling, and a multitude of black people of every description chained together, every one of their countenances expressing dejection and sorrow, I no longer doubted my fate. Quite overpowered with horror and anguish, I fell motionless on the deck and fainted. When I recovered a little, I found some black people about me, and I believe some were those who had brought me on board and had been receiving their pay. They talked to me in order to cheer me up, but all in vain. I asked them if we were not to be eaten by those white men with horrible looks, red faces and long hair. They told me I was not.

I took a little down my palate, which, instead of reviving me as they thought it would, threw me into the greatest consternation at the strange feeling it produced, having never tasted such liquor before. Soon after this, the blacks who had brought me on board went off and left me abandoned to despair.

I now saw myself deprived of all chance of returning to my

Source: *The Interesting Narrative of the Life of Olaudah Equiano or Gustavus Vassa the African* (London, 1789).

native country or even the least glimpse of hope of gaining the shore, which I now considered as friendly. I even wished for my former slavery in preference to my present situation, which was filled with horrors of every kind.

There I received such a salutation in my nostrils as I had never experienced in my life. With the loathesomeness of the stench and the crying together, I became so sick and low that I was not able to eat, nor had I the least desire to taste anything. I now wished for the last friend, Death, to relieve me.

Soon, to my grief, two of the white men offered me eatables and on my refusing to eat, one of them held me fast by the hands and laid me across the windlass and tied my feet while the other flogged me severely. I had never experienced anything of this kind before. If I could have gotten over the nettings, I would have jumped over the side, but I could not. The crew used to watch very closely those of us who were not chained down to the decks, lest we should leap into the water. I have seen some of these poor African prisoners most severely cut for attempting to do so, and hourly whipped for not eating. This indeed was often the case with myself.

I inquired of these what was to be done with us. They gave me to understand we were to be carried to these white people's country to work for them. I then was a little revived, and thought if it were no worse than working, my situation was not so desperate. But still I feared that I should be put to death, the white people looked and acted in so savage a manner. I have never seen among my people such instances of brutal cruelty, and this not only shown towards us blacks, but also to some of the whites themselves.

One white man in particular I saw, when we were permitted to be on deck, flogged so unmercifully with a large rope near the foremast that he died in consequence of it, and they tossed him over the side as they would have done a brute. This made me fear these people the more, and I expected nothing less than to be treated in the same manner.

I asked them if these people had no country, but lived in this hollow place? They told me they did not but came from a distant land. "Then," said I, "how comes it that in all our country we never heard of them?"

They told me because they lived so far off. I then asked where were their women? Had they any like themselves? I was told they had.

"And why do we not see them" I asked. They answered, "Because they were left behind."

I asked how the vessel would go? They told me they could not tell, but there was cloth put upon the masts by the help of the ropes I saw, and then vessels went on, and the white men had some spell or magic they put in the water when they liked in order to stop the vessel when they liked.

I was exceedingly amazed at this account, and really thought they were spirits. I therefore wished much to be from amongst them, for I expected they would sacrifice me. But my wishes were in vain—for we were so quartered that it was impossible for us to make our escape.

At last, when the ship we were in had got in all her cargo, they made ready with many fearful noises, and we were all put under deck, so that we could not see how they managed the vessel.

The stench of the hold while we were on the coast was so intolerably loathsome, that it was dangerous to remain there for any time . . . some of us had been permitted to stay on the deck for the fresh air. But now that the whole ship's cargo were confined together, it became absolutely pestilential. The closeness of the place and the heat of the climate, added to the number of the ship, which was so crowded that each had scarcely room to turn himself, almost suffocated us.

This produced copious perspirations so that the air became unfit for respiration from a variety of loathsome smells, and brought on a sickness among the slaves, of which many died—thus falling victims of the improvident avarice, as I may call it, of their purchasers. This wretched situation was again aggravated by the galling of the chains, which now became insupportable, and the filth of the necessary tubs [toilets] into which the children often fell and were almost suffocated. The shrieks of the women and the groans of the dying rendered the whole a scene of horror almost inconceivable.

Happily perhaps for myself, I was soon reduced so low that it was necessary to keep me almost always on deck and from my extreme youth I was not put into fetters. In this situation I expected every hour to share the fate of my companions, some of whom were almost daily brought upon the deck at the point of death, which I began to hope would soon put an end to my miseries. Often did I think many of the inhabitants of the deep much more happy than myself. I envied them the freedom they enjoyed, and as often wished I could change my condition for theirs. Every circumstance I met with, served only to render my state more painful and heightened my apprehensions and my opinion of the cruelty of the whites.

One day, when we had a smooth sea and moderate wind, two of my wearied countrymen who were chained together (I was near them at the time), preferring death to such a life of misery, somehow made through the nettings and jumped into the sea. Immediately another quite dejected fellow, who on account of his illness was suffered to be out of irons, followed their example. I believe many more would very soon have done the same if they had not been prevented by the ship's crew, who were instantly alarmed. Those of us that were the most active were in a moment put down under the deck, and there was such a noise and confusion among the people of the ship as I never heard before to stop her and get the boat out to go after the slaves. However, two of the wretches were drowned, but they got the other and afterwards flogged him unmercifully for thus attempting to prefer death to slavery.

I can now relate hardships which are inseparable from this accursed trade. Many a time we were near suffocation from the want of fresh air, which we were often without for whole days together. This, and the stench of the necessary tubs, carried off many.

7
Alexander Falconbridge

"THE MEN NEGROES ... ARE ... FASTENED TOGETHER ... BY HANDCUFFS"

Alexander Falconbridge, a surgeon aboard slave ships and later the governor of a British colony for freed slaves in Sierra Leone, offers a vivid account of Middle Passage.

From the time of the arrival of the ships to their departure, which is usually about three months, scarce a day passes without some Negroes being purchased and carried on board; sometimes in small and sometimes in large numbers. The whole number taken on board depends on circumstances. In a voyage I once made, our stock of merchandise was exhausted in the purchase of about 380 Negroes, which was expected to have procured 500. . . .

The unhappy wretches thus disposed of are bought by the black traders at fairs, which are held for that purpose, at the distance of upwards of two hundred miles from the sea coast; and these fairs are said to be supplied from an interior part of the country. Many Negroes, upon being questioned relative to the places of their nativity, have asserted that they have travelled during the revolution of several moons (their usual method of calculating time) before they have reached the places where they were purchased by the black traders.

At these fairs, which are held at uncertain periods, but generally every six weeks, several thousands are frequently exposed to sale who had been collected from all parts of the country for a very considerable distance around. . . . During one of my voyages, the black traders brought down, in different canoes, from twelve to fifteen hundred Negroes who had been purchased at one fair. They consisted chiefly of men and boys, the women seldom exceeding a

Source: Alexander Falconbridge, *An Account of the Slave Trade on the Coast of Africa* (London, 1788).

third of the whole number. From forty to two hundred Negroes are generally purchased at a time by the black traders, according to the opulence of the buyer, and consist of all ages, from a month to sixty years and upwards. Scarcely any age or situation is deemed an exception, the price being proportionable. Women sometimes form a part of them, who happen to be so far advanced in their pregnancy as to be delivered during their journey from the fairs to the coast; and I have frequently seen instances of deliveries on board ship. . . .

When the Negroes, whom the black traders have to dispose of, are shown to the European purchasers, they first examine them relative to their age. They then minutely inspect their persons and inquire into the state of their health; if they are inflicted with any disease or are deformed or have bad eyes or teeth; if they are lame or weak in the joints or distorted in the back or of a slender make or narrow in the chest; in short, if they have been ill or are afflicted in any manner so as to render them incapable of much labor. If any of the foregoing defects are discovered in them they are rejected. But if approved of, they are generally taken on board the ship the same evening. The purchaser has liberty to return on the following morning, but not afterwards, such as upon re-examination are found exceptionable. . . .

Near the mainmast a partition is constructed of boards which reaches athwart the ship. This division is called a barricado. It is about eight feet in height and is made to project about two feet over the sides of the ship. In this barricado there is a door at which a sentinel is placed during the time the Negroes are permitted to come upon the deck. It serves to keep the different sexes apart; and as there are small holes in it, where blunderbusses are fixed and sometimes a cannon, it is found very convenient for quelling the insurrections that now and then happen. . . .

The men Negroes, on being brought aboard the ship, are immediately fastened together, two and two, by handcuffs on their wrists and by irons riveted on their legs. They are then sent down between the decks and placed in an apartment partitioned off for that purpose. The women also are placed in a separate apartment between the decks, but without being ironed. An adjoining room on the same deck is appointed for the boys. Thus they are all placed in different apartments.

But at the same time, however, they are frequently stowed so close, as to admit of no other position than lying on their sides. Nor with the height between decks, unless directly under the grating, permit the indulgence of an erect posture; especially where there are platforms, which is generally the case. These platforms are a kind of shelf, about eight or nine feet in breadth, extending from the side of the ship toward the centre. They are placed nearly midway between the decks, at the distance of two or three feet from each deck. Upon these the Negroes are stowed in the same manner as they are on the deck underneath.

In each of the apartments are placed three or four large buckets, of a conical form, nearly two feet in diameter at the bottom and only one foot at the top and in depth of about twenty-eight inches, to which, when necessary, the Negroes have recourse. It often happens that those who are placed at a distance from the buckets, in endeavoring to get to them, tumble over their companions, in consequence of their being shackled. These accidents, although unavoidable, are productive of continual quarrels in which some of them are always bruised. In this distressed situation, unable to proceed and prevented from getting to the tubs, they desist from the attempt; and as the necessities of nature are not to be resisted, ease themselves as they lie. This becomes a fresh source of boils and disturbances and tends to render the condition of the poor captive wretches still more uncomfortable. The nuisance arising from these circumstances is not infrequently increased by the tubs being too small for the purpose intended and their being emptied but once every day. The rule for doing so, however, varies in different ships according to the attention paid to the health and convenience of the slaves by the captain.

About eight o'clock in the morning the Negroes are generally brought upon deck. Their irons being examined, a long chain, which is locked to a ring-bolt fixed in the deck, is run through the rings of the shackles of the men and then locked to another ring-bolt fixed also in the deck. By this means fifty or sixty and sometimes more are fastened to one chain in order to prevent them from rising or endeavoring to escape. If the weather proves favorable they are permitted to remain in that situation till four or five in the afternoon when they are disengaged from the chain and sent below.

The diet of the Negroes while on board, consists chiefly of horse beans boiled to the consistency of a pulp; of boiled yams and rice and sometimes a small quantity of beef or pork. The latter are frequently taken from the provisions laid in for the sailors. They sometimes make use of a sauce composed of palm-oil mixed with flour, water and pepper, which the sailors call slabber-sauce. Yams are the favorite food of the Eboe [Ibo] or Bight Negroes, and rice or corn of those from the Gold or Windward Coast; each preferring the produce of their native soil. . . .

They are commonly fed twice a day; about eight o'clock in the morning and four in the afternoon. In most ships they are only fed with their own food once a day. Their food is served up to them in tubs about the size of a small water bucket. They are placed round these tubs, in companies of ten to each tub, out of which they feed themselves with wooden spoons. These they soon lose and when they are not allowed others they feed themselves with their hands. In favorable weather they are fed upon deck but in bad weather their food is given them below. Numberless quarrels take place among them during their meals; more especially when they are put upon short allowance, which frequently happens if the passage from the coast of Guinea to the West Indies islands proves of unusual length. In that case, the weak are obliged to be content with a very scanty portion. Their allowance of water is about half a pint each at every meal. It is handed round in a bucket and given to each Negro in a pannekin, a small utensil with a straight handle, somewhat similar to a sauce-boat. However, when the ships approach the islands with a favourable breeze, the slaves are no longer restricted.

Upon the Negroes refusing to take sustenance, I have seen coals of fire, glowing hot, put on a shovel and placed so near their lips as to scorch and burn them. And this has been accompanied with threats of forcing them to swallow the coals if they any longer persisted in refusing to eat. These means have generally had the desired effect. I have also been credibly informed that a certain captain in the slave-trade, poured melted lead on such of his Negroes as obstinately refused their food.

Exercise being deemed necessary for the preservation of their health they are sometimes obliged to dance when the weather will permit their coming on deck. If they go about it reluctantly or do not move with agility, they are flogged; a person standing by them all the time with a cat-o'-nine-tails in his hands for the purpose. Their music, upon these occasions, consists of a drum, sometimes with only one head; and when that is worn out they make use of the bottom of one of the tubs before described. The poor wretches are frequently compelled to sing also; but when they do so, their songs are generally, as may naturally be expected, melancholy lamentations of their exile from their native country.

The women are furnished with beads for the purpose of affording them some diversion. But this end is generally defeated by the squabbles which are occasioned in consequence of their stealing from each other.

On board some ships the common sailors are allowed to have intercourse with such of the black women whose consent they can procure. And some of them have been known to take the inconstancy of their paramours so much to heart as to leap overboard and drown themselves. The officers are permitted to indulge their passions among them at pleasure and sometimes are guilty of such excesses as disgrace human nature. . . .

The hardships and inconveniences suffered by the Negroes during the passage are scarcely to be enumerated or conceived. They are far more violently affected by seasickness than Europeans. It frequently terminates in death, especially among the women. But the exclusion of fresh air is among the most intolerable. For the purpose of admitting this needful refreshment, most of the ships in the slave trade are provided, between the decks, with five or sick air-ports on each side of the ship of about five inches in length and four in breadth. In addition, some ships, but not one in twenty, have what they denominate wind-sails. But whenever the sea is rough and the rain heavy is becomes necessary to shut these and every other conveyance by which the air is admitted. The fresh air being thus excluded, the Negroes' rooms soon grow intolerable hot. The confined air, rendered noxious by the effluvia exhaled from their bodies and being repeatedly breathed, soon produces fevers and fluxes which generally carries of great numbers of them.

During the voyages I made, I was frequently witness to the fatal effects of this exclusion of fresh air. I will give one instance, as it serves to convey some idea, though a very faint one, of their terrible sufferings. . . . Some wet and blowing weather having occasioned the port-holes to be shut and the grating to be covered, fluxes and fevers among the Negroes ensued. While they were in this situation, I frequently went down among them till at length their room became so extremely hot as to be only bearable for a very short time. But the excessive heat was not the only thing that rendered their situation intolerable. The deck, that is the floor of their rooms, was so covered with the blood and mucus which had proceeded from them in consequence of the flux, that it resembled a slaughter-house. It is not in the power of the human imagination to picture a situation more dreadful or disgusting. Numbers of the slaves having fainted, they were carried upon deck where several of them died and the rest with great difficulty were restored. . . .

As very few of the Negroes can so far brook the loss of their liberty and the hardships they endure, they are ever on the watch to take advantage of the least negligence in their oppressors. Insurrections are frequently the consequence; which are seldom expressed without much bloodshed. Sometimes these are successful and the whole ship's company is cut off. They are likewise always ready to seize every opportunity for committing some acts of desperation to free themselves from their miserable state and notwithstanding the restraints which are laid, they often succeed.

Part 3

ARRIVAL:

"Dere's No Hidin' Place Down Here"

In 1806, a year before the United States and Britain outlawed the African slave trade, George Pickard, an English physician, witnessed the sale of a newly-arrived boatload of enslaved Africans in the West Indies. To the white settlers, he wrote, "it seemed a day of feasting and hilarity, but to the poor Africans it was a period of heavy grief and affliction; for they were to be sold as beasts of burden—torn from each other—and widely dispersed."

The terrors of the Middle Passage were followed by another series of shocks. The "unpitied sable beings" were put on public auction. The purchasers, observed Pickard, "handled and inspected them, with as little concern as if they had been examining cattle." "They turned them about, felt them, viewed their shapes and limbs, and looked into their mouths, made them jump and throw out their arms, and subjected them to all the means of trial as if dealing for a horse or other brute animal."

Family ties were often disregarded by the purchasers. One slave, Pickard wrote, told to stand up, refused, and "sunk his chin upon his breast and hung his head." He pointed to an African woman, "held up two fingers to the auctioneer, and implored the multitude in anxious suppliant gestures. . . . which seemed to say—'Let us be sold together.'"

8
Olaudah Equiano

"DREAD AND TREMBLING"

Olaudah Equiano offers a first hand account of his arrival in the West Indies in 1756.

As the vessel drew nearer, we plainly saw the harbor and other ships of different kinds and sizes and we soon anchored amongst them off Bridgetown. Many merchants and planters came on board.... They put us in separate parcels and examined us attentively. They also made us jump, and pointed to the land, signifying we were to go there. We thought by this we should be eaten by these ugly men, as they appeared to us. When soon after we were all put down under the deck again, there was much dread and trembling among us and nothing but bitter cries to be heard all the night from the apprehensions. At last the white people got some old slaves from the land to pacify us. They told us we were not to be eaten, but to work, and were soon to go on land, where we should see many of our country people. This report eased us much, and sure enough, soon after we landed, there came to us Africans of all languages.

We were conducted immediately to the merchant's yard, where we were all pent up together, like so many sheep in a fold, without regard to sex or age. As every object was new to me, everything I saw filled me with surprise. What struck me first was that the houses were built with bricks and stones, and in every respect different from those I had seen in Africa, but I was still more astonished to see people on horseback. I did not know what this could mean, and indeed I thought these people were full of nothing but magical arts. While I was in this astonishment, one of my fellow prisoners spoke to a countryman of his about the horses who said

Source: *The Interesting Narrative of the Life of Olaudah Equiano or Gustavus Vassa the African* (London, 1789).

they were the same kind they had in their country. I understood them, though they were from a distant part of Africa and I thought it odd I had not seen any horses there; but afterwards when I came to converse with different Africans, I found they had many horses amongst them, and much larger than those I then saw.

We were not many days in the merchant's custody, before we were sold after their usual manner.... On a signal given, (as the beat of a drum), buyers rush at once into the yard where the slaves are confined, and make a choice of that parcel they like best. The noise and clamor with which this is attended, and the eagerness visible in the countenances of the buyers, serve not a little to increase the apprehension of terrified Africans ... In this manner, without scruple, are relations and friends separated, most of them never to see each other again. I remember in the vessel in which I was brought over ... there were several brothers who, in the sale, were sold in different lots; and it was very moving on this occasion, to see and hear their cries in parting.

9
Alexander Falconbridge

"VARIOUS DECEPTIONS ARE USED IN THE DISPOSAL OF SICK SLAVES"

Alexander Falconbridge describes the reaction of enslaved Africans to their sale.

When the ships arrive in the West Indies (the chief mart for this inhuman merchandize), the slaves are disposed as I have before observed by different methods. Sometimes the mode of disposal is that of selling them by what is termed a scramble, and a day is soon fixed for that purpose. Previously the sick or refuse slaves, of which there are frequently many, are usually conveyed on shore and sold at a tavern, by vendue or public auction. These in general are purchased . . . upon speculation, at so low a price as five or six dollars a head. I was informed by a mulatto woman that she purchased a sick slave at Grenada, upon speculation, for the small sum of one dollar, as the poor wretch was apparently dying of the flux. It seldom happens that any who are carried ashore in the emaciated state to which they are generally reduced by that disorder long survive after their landing. I once saw sixteen conveyed on shore and sold in the foregoing manner, the whole of whom died before I left the island. Sometimes the captains march their slaves through the town at which they intend to dispose of them, and then place them in rows where they are examined and purchased.

The mode of selling them by scramble having fallen under my observation the oftenest, I shall be more particular in describing it. Being some years ago, at one of the islands in the West Indies, I was witness to a sale by scramble, where about 250 Negroes were sold. Upon this occasion all the Negroes scrambled for bear an

Source: Alexander Falconbridge, *An Account of the Slave Trade on the Coast of Africa* (London, 1788).

equal price; which is agreed upon between the captains and the purchasers before the sale begins. On a day appointed, the Negroes were landed and placed together in a large yard belonging to the merchants to whom the ship was consigned. As soon as the hour agreed on arrived, the doors of the yard were suddenly thrown open and in rushed a considerable number of purchasers, with all the ferocity of brutes. Some instantly seized such of the Negroes as they could conveniently lay hold of with their hands. Others being prepared with several handkerchiefs tied together, encircled as many as they were able. While others, by means of a rope, effected the same purpose. It is scarcely possible to describe the confusion of which this mode of selling is productive. It likewise causes much animosity among the purchasers who not infrequently fall out and quarrel with each other. The poor astonished Negroes were so terrified by these proceedings, that several of them, through fear climbed over the walls of the courtyard and ran wild about the town, but were soon hunted down and retaken. . . .

Various deceptions are used in the disposal of sick slaves and many of these must excite in every humane mind the liveliest sensations of horror. I have been well informed that a Liverpool captain boasted of his having cheated some Jews by the following stratagem. A lot of slaves afflicted with the flux, being about to be landed for sale, he directed the ship's surgeons to stop the anus of each of them with oakum. Thus prepared they were landed and taken to the accustomed place of sale, where, being unable to stand but for a very short time, they were usually permitted to sit. The buyers, when they examined them, oblige them to stand up in order to see if there be any discharge; and when they do not perceive this appearance they consider it as a symptom of recovery. In the present instance, such an appearance being prevented, the bargain was struck and the slaves were accordingly sold. But it was not long before discovery ensued. The excruciating pain which the prevention of a discharge of such an acrimonious nature occasioned, not being able to be borne by the poor wretches, the temporary obstruction was removed and the deluded purchasers were speedily convinced of the imposition.

Part 4

CONDITIONS OF LIFE:
"We Raise de Wheat, Dey Gib Us de Corn"

In 1852, the New York Times *commissioned Frederick Law Olmsted to travel through the Cotton Kingdom and conduct an objective investigation of slavery. His assignment: to assess slaves' working conditions, the type of food they ate, the use of the whip by masters and overseers, and the amount of free time available to slaves. For fourteen months, Olmsted crisscrossed the South on horseback, stagecoach, and train; then, between 1856 and 1860, he published three volumes of his observations. He depicted slavery as a wasteful and inefficient system, which degraded labor, exhausted soil, and deprived slaves of any incentives to work hard. He charged that planters, fearful of sabotage or carelessness, provided slaves with only simple, heavy implements, and depicted slave labor as crude, brutish work.*

Historians now know that Olmsted's portrait of slavery was seriously distorted. Far from being inefficient, slave labor was highly productive. While cultivating cotton, rice, and tobacco was hard, backbreaking work, it also required a high degree of care and skill. Moreover, many slaves served as skilled craftsmen, working as blacksmiths, butchers, carpenters, coopers, bricklayers, metal workers, tanners, weavers, and wheelwrights.

This chapter's selections offer graphic portraits of life under slavery. From these eyewitness accounts of slavery, it is possible to reach our own conclusions about slaves' working conditions and their diet, clothing, and housing.

10
Solomon Northrup

"THERE IS NO SUCH THING AS REST"

Solomon Northrup was a free black who was kidnapped in New York and sold into slavery for twelve years. He was finally returned to freedom through the efforts of New York's governor. In the following selection he describes how cotton was raised on his Louisiana plantation.

The hands are required to be in the cotton field as soon as it is light in the morning, and, with the exception of ten or fifteen minutes, which is given them at noon to swallow their allowance of cold bacon, they are not permitted to be a moment idle until it is too dark to see, and when the moon is full, they oftentimes labor till the middle of the night. They do not dare to stop even at dinner time, nor return to the quarters, however late it be, until the order to halt is given by the driver.

The day's work over in the field, the baskets are "toted," or in other words, carried to the gin-house, where the cotton is weighed. No matter how fatigued and weary he may be—no matter how much he longs for sleep and rest—a slave never approaches the gin-house with his basket of cotton but with fear. If it falls short in weight—if he has not performed the full task appointed him, he knows that he must suffer. And if he has exceeded it by ten or twenty pounds, in all probability his master will measure the next day's task accordingly. So, whether he has too little or too much, his approach to the gin-house is always with fear and trembling. Most frequently they have too little, and therefore it is they who are not anxious to leave the field. After weighing, follow the whippings; and then the baskets are carried to the cotton house, and their contents stored away like hay, all hands being sent in to tramp it down. If the cotton is not dry, instead of taking it to the

Source: *Twelve Years a Slave: Narrative of Solomon Northrup* (Auburn, N.Y., 1853).

gin-house at once, it is laid upon platforms, two feet high, and some three times as wide, covered with boards or plank, with narrow walks running between them.

This done, the labor of the day is not yet ended, by any means. Each one must then attend to his respective chores. One feeds the mules, another the swine—another cuts the wood, and so forth; besides, the packing is all done by candle light. Finally, at a late hour, they reach the quarters, sleepy and overcome with the long day's toil. Then a fire must be kindled in the cabin, the corn ground in the small hand-mill, and supper, and dinner for the next day in the field, prepared. All that is allowed them is corn and bacon, which is given out at the corncrib and smoke-house every Sunday morning. Each one receives, as his weekly allowance, three and a half pounds of bacon, and corn enough to make a peck of meal. That is all—no tea, coffee, sugar, and with the exception of a very scanty sprinkling now and then, no salt. . . .

An hour before daylight the horn is blown. Then the slaves arouse, prepare their breakfast, fill a gourd with water, in another deposit their dinner of cold bacon and corn cake, and hurry to the field again. It is an offense invariably followed by a flogging, to be found at the quarters after daybreak. Then the fears and labors of another day begin; and until its close there is no such thing as rest. . . .

In the month of January, generally, the fourth and last picking is completed. Then commences the harvesting of corn. . . . Ploughing, planting, picking cotton, gathering the corn, and pulling and burning stalks, occupies the whole of the four seasons of the year. Drawing and cutting wood, pressing cotton, fattening and killing hogs are but incidental labors.

11
Charles Ball

"THE GENERAL FEATURES OF SLAVERY ARE THE SAME EVERYWHERE"

For forty years, Charles Ball toiled as a slave in Maryland, South Carolina, and Georgia, and, according to his autobiography, managed to escape twice. In the following selection, he describes the regimen on a tobacco plantation.

In Maryland and Virginia, although the slaves are treated with so much rigour, and oftimes with so much cruelty, I have seen instances of the greatest tenderness of feeling on the part of their owners. I, myself, had three masters in Maryland, and I cannot say now, even after having resided so many years in a state where slavery is not tolerated, that either of them (except the last, who sold me to the Georgians, and was an unfeeling man,) used me worse than they had a moral right to do, regarding me merely as an article of property, and not entitled to any rights as a man, political or civil. My mistresses, in Maryland, were all good women; and the mistress of my wife, in whose kitchen I spent my Sundays and many of my nights, for several years, was a lady of most benevolent and kindly feelings. She was a true friend to me, and I shall always venerate her memory. . . .

If the proprietors of the soil in Maryland and Virginia, were skillful cultivators—had their lands in good condition—and kept no more slaves on each estate, than would be sufficient to work the soil in a proper manner, and kept up the repairs of the place—the condition of the coloured people would not be, by any means, a comparatively unhappy one. I am convinced, that in nine cases in ten, the hardships and suffering of the coloured population of lower Virginia, are attributable to the poverty and distress of its

---

Source: Charles Ball, *Fifty Years in Chains; or, the Life of an American Slave* (New York, 1858).

owners. In many instances, an estate scarcely yields enough to feed and clothe the slaves in a comfortable manner, without allowing anything for the support of the master and family; but it is obvious, that the family must first be supported, and the slaves must be content with the surplus—and this, on a poor, old, worn out tobacco plantation, is often very small, and wholly inadequate to the comfortable sustenance of the hands, as they are called. There, in many places, nothing is allowed to the poor Negro, but his peck of corn per week, without the sauce of a salt herring, or even a little salt itself. . . .

The general features of slavery are the same everywhere; but the utmost rigour of the system, is only to be met with, on the cotton plantations of Carolina and Georgia, or in the rice fields which skirt the deep swamps and morasses of the southern rivers. In the tobacco fields of Maryland and Virginia, great cruelties are practiced—not so frequently by the owners, as by the overseers of the slaves; but yet, the tasks are not so excessive as in the cotton region, nor is the press of labour so incessant throughout the year. It is true, that from the period when the tobacco plants are set in the field, there is no resting time until it is housed; but it is planted out about the first of May, and must be cut and taken out of the field before the frost comes. After it is hung and dried, the labor of stripping and preparing it for the hogshead in leaf, or of manufacturing it into twist, is comparatively a work of leisure and ease. Besides, on almost every plantation the hands are able to complete the work of preparing the tobacco by January, and sometimes earlier; so that the winter months, form some sort of respite from the toils of the year. The people are obliged, it is true, to occupy themselves in cutting wood for the house, making rails and repairing fences, and in clearing new land, to raise the tobacco plants for the next year; but as there is usually time enough, and to spare, for the completion of all this work, before the season arrives for setting the plants in the field; the men are seldom flogged much, unless they are very lazy or negligent, and the women are allowed to remain in the house, in the very cold, snowy, or rainy weather. . . .

In Maryland I never knew a mistress or a young mistress, who would not listen to the complaints of the slaves. It is true, we were always obliged to approach the door of the mansion, with our hats in our hands, and the most subdued and beseeching language in our mouths—but, in return, we generally received words of kindness, and very often a redress of our grievances; though I have known very great ladies, who would never grant any request from the plantation hands, but always referred them and their petitions to their master, under a pretence, that they could not meddle with things that did not belong to the house. The mistresses of the great families, generally gave mild language to the slaves; though they sometimes sent for the overseer and had them severely flogged; but I have never heard any mistress, in either Maryland or Virginia, indulge in the low, vulgar and profane vituperations, of which I was myself the object, in Georgia, for many years, whenever I came into the presence of my mistress. Flogging—though often severe and excruciating in Maryland, is not practiced with the order, regularity and system, to which it is often reduced in the South. On the Potomac, if a slave gives offence, he is generally chastised on the spot, in the field where he is at work, as the overseer always carried a whip—sometimes a twisted cow-hide, sometimes a kind of horse-whip, and very often a simple hickory switch or gad, cut in the adjoining woods. For stealing meat, or other provisions, or for any of the higher offences, the slaves are stripped, tied up by the hands—sometimes by the thumbs—and whipped at the quarter—but many times, on a large tobacco plantation, there is not more than one of these regular whippings in a week—though on others, where the master happens to be a bad man, or a drunkard—the back of the unhappy Maryland slaves, is seamed with scars from his neck to his hips.

12
Josiah Henson

"WE LODGED IN LOG HUTS"

Josiah Henson spent thirty years on a plantation in Montgomery County, Maryland before he escaped slavery and became a Methodist preacher, abolitionist, lecturer, and founder of a cooperative colony of former slaves in Canada. His memoirs, published in 1849, provided Harriet Beecher Stowe with her model of Uncle Tom.

My earliest employments were, to carry buckets of water to the men at work, and to hold a horse-plough, used for weeding between the rows of corn. As I grew older and taller, I was entrusted with the care of master's saddle-horse. Then a hoe was put into my hands, and I was soon required to do the day's work of a man; and it was not long before I could do it, at least as well as my associates in misery.

A description of the everyday life of a slave on a Southern plantation illustrates the character and habits of the slave and the slaveholder, created and perpetuated by their relative position. The principal food of those upon my master's plantation consisted of corn-meal and salt herrings; to which was added in summer a little buttermilk, and the few vegetables which each might raise for himself and his family, on the little piece of ground which was assigned to him for the purpose, called a truck-patch.

In ordinary times we had two regular meals in a day: breakfast at twelve o'clock, after laboring from daylight, and supper when the work of the remainder of the day was over. In harvest season we had three. Our dress was of tow-cloth; for the children, nothing but a shirt; for the older ones a pair of pantaloons or a gown in addition, according to the sex. Besides these, in the winter

Source: *"Uncle Tom's Story of His Life": An Autobiography of the Rev. Josiah Henson* (London, 1877).

a round jacket or overcoat, a wool-hat once in two or three years, for the males, and a pair of coarse shoes once a year.

We lodged in log huts, and on the bare ground. Wooden floors were an unknown luxury. In a single room were huddled, like cattle, ten or a dozen persons, men, women, and children. All ideas of refinement and decency were, of course, out of the question. We had neither bedsteads, nor furniture of any description. Our beds were collections of straw and old rags, thrown down in the corners and boxed in with boards; a single blanket the only covering. Our favourite way of sleeping, however, was on a plank, our heads raised on an old jacket and our feet toasting before the smouldering fire. The wind whistled and the rain and snow blew in through the cracks, and the damp earth soaked in the moisture till the floor was miry as a pig-sty. Such were our houses. In these wretched hovels were we penned at night, and fed by day; here were the children born and the sick—neglected.

13
Francis Henderson

"MY BEDSTEAD CONSISTED OF A BOARD WIDE ENOUGH TO SLEEP ON"

Francis Henderson was nineteen when he managed to escape from a slave plantation outside of Washington, D.C., in 1841. Here, he describes conditions on his plantation.

Our houses were but log huts—the tops partly open—ground floor—rain would come through. My aunt was quite an old woman, and had been sick several years; in rains I have seen her moving from one part of the house to the other, and rolling her bedclothes about to try to keep dry—everything would be dirty and muddy. I lived in the house with my aunt. My bed and bedstead consisted of a board wide enough to sleep on—one end on a stool, the other placed near the fire. My pillow consisted of my jacket—my covering was whatever I could get. My bedtick was the board itself. And this was the way the single men slept—but we were comfortable in this way of sleeping, being used to it. I only remember having but one blanket from my owners up to the age of nineteen, when I ran away.

Our allowance was given weekly—a peck of sifted corn meal, a dozen and a half herrings, two and a half pounds of pork. Some of the boys would eat this up in three days—then they had to steal, or they could not perform their daily tasks. They would visit the hog-pen, sheep-pen, and granaries. I do not remember one slave but who stole some things—they were driven to it as a matter of necessity. I myself did this—many a time have I, with others, run among the stumps in chase of a sheep, that we might have something to eat.... In regard to cooking, sometimes many have to cook at one fire, and before all could get to the fire to bake hoe cakes, the

---

Source: Benjamin Drew, *A North-Side View of Slavery* (Boston, 1856).

overseer's horn would sound: then they must go at any rate. Many a time I have gone along eating a piece of bread and meat, or herring broiled on the coals—I never sat down at a table to eat except at harvest time, all the time I was a slave. In harvest time, the cooking is done at the great house, as the hands they have are wanted in the field. This was more like people, and we liked it, for we sat down then at meals. In the summer we had one pair of linen trousers given us—nothing else; every fall, one pair of woolen pantaloons, one woolen jacket, and two cotton shirts.

My master had four sons in his family. They all left except one, who remained to be a driver. He would often come to the field and accuse the slave of having taken so and so. If we denied it, he would whip the grown-up ones to make them own it. Many a time, when we didn't know he was anywhere around, he would be in the woods watching us—first thing we would know, he would be sitting on the fence looking down upon us, and if any had been idle, the young master would visit him with blows. I have known him to kick my aunt, an old woman who had raised and nursed him, and I have seen him punish my sisters awfully with hickories from the woods.

The slaves are watched by the patrols, who ride about to try to catch them off the quarters, especially at the house of a free person of color. I have known the slaves to stretch clothes lines across the street, high enough to let the horse pass, but not the rider; then the boys would run, and the patrols in full chase would be thrown off by running against the lines. The patrols are poor white men, who live by plundering and stealing, getting rewards for runaways, and setting up little shops on the public roads. They will take whatever the slaves steal, paying in money, whiskey, or whatever the slaves want. They take pigs, sheep, wheat, corn—anything that's raised they encourage the slaves to steal: these they take to market next day. It's all speculation—all a matter of self-interest, and when the slaves run away, these same traders catch them if they can, to get the reward. If the slave threatens to expose his traffic, he does not care—for the slave's word is good for nothing—it would not be taken.

14
Jacob Stroyer

"MOST OF THE CABINS ... WERE BUILT ... TO CONTAIN TWO FAMILIES"

One of fifteen children, Jacob Stroyer was born on a planta-
tion twenty-eight miles from Columbia, South Carolina, in
1849. After the Civil War he became an African Methodist
Episcopal minister, serving in Salem, Massachusetts.

Most of the cabins in the time of slavery were built so as to
contain two families; some had partitions, while others had none.
When there were no partitions each family would fit up its own
part as it could; sometimes they got old boards and nailed them
up, stuffing the cracks with rags; when they could not get boards
they hung up old clothes. When the family increased, the children
all slept together, both boys and girls, until one got married; then
a part of another cabin was assigned to that one, but the rest would
have to remain with their mother and father, as in childhood,
unless they could get with some of their relatives or friends who
had small families, or unless they were sold; but of course the rules
of modesty were held in some degrees by the slaves, while it could
not be expected that they could entertain the highest degree of it,
on account of their condition. A portion of the time the young men
slept in the apartment known as the kitchen, and the young
women slept in the room with their mother and father. The two
families had to use one fireplace. One who was accustomed to the
way in which the slaves lived in their cabins could tell as soon as
he entered whether they were friendly or not, for when they did not
agree, the fires of the two families did not meet on the hearth, but
there was a vacancy between them, that was a sign of disagree-
ment. In a case of this kind, when either of the families stole a hog,
cow or sheep from the master, he had to carry it to some of his fam-

Source: Jacob Stroyer, *My Life in the South* (enlarged edition; Salem, Mass., 1898)

ily, for fear of being betrayed by the other family. On one occasion a man, who lived with one unfriendly, stole a hog, killed it and carried some of the meat home. He was seen by some one of the other family, who reported him to the overseer, and he gave the man a severe whipping. . . .

No doubt you would like to know how the slaves could sleep in their cabins in summer, when it was so very warm. When it was too warm for them to sleep comfortably, they all slept under trees until it grew too cool, that is along in the month of October. Then they took up their beds and walked.

15
James Martin

"THE SLAVES ARE PUT IN STALLS
LIKE ... CATTLE"

James Martin, born on a Virginia plantation in 1847, was ninety years old when he was interviewed by the Works Progress Administration in 1937. After the Civil War he moved to Texas, where he served in the 9th U.S. Cavalry and later worked as a cowboy. Here, he describes a slave auction.

The slaves are put in stalls like the pens they use for cattle—a man and his wife with a child on each arm. And there's a curtain, sometimes just a sheet over the front of the stall, so the bidders can't see the "stock" too soon. The overseer's standin' just outside with a big black snake whip and a pepperbox pistol in his belt. Across the square a little piece, there's a big platform with steps leadin' to it.

Then, they pulls up the curtain, and the bidders is crowdin' around. Them in back can't see, so the overseer drives the slaves out to the platform, and he tells the ages of the slaves and what they can do. They have white gloves there, and one of the bidders takes a pair of gloves and rubs his fingers over a man's teeth, and he says to the overseer, "You call this buck twenty years old? Why there's cut worms in his teeth. He's forty years old, if he's a day." So they knock this buck down for a thousand dollars. They calls the men "bucks" and the women "wenches."

When the slaves is on the platform—what they calls the "block"—the overseer yells, "Tom or Jason, show the bidders how you walk." Then, the slave steps across the platform, and the biddin' starts.

Source: George P. Rawick, ed., *The American Slave: A Composite Autobiography* (Westport, Conn., 1972), Texas Narr., Vol.5, 62-65.

At these slave auctions, the overseer yells, "Say, you bucks and wenches, get in your hole. Come out here." Then, he makes 'em hop, he makes 'em trot, he makes 'em jump. "How much," he yells, "for this buck? A thousand? Eleven hundred? Twelve hundred dollars?" Then the bidders makes offers accordin' to size and build.

Part 5

CHILDHOOD:

"Like a Motherless Child"

As they remembered their lives in bondage, former slaves invariably recalled a moment in their childhood when they were first forced to confront the harsh realities of slavery. For one former Louisiana slave that moment came when her mistress whipped her for saying "to missis, 'My mother sent me.' We were not allowed to call our mammies 'mother.' It was too near the way of the white folks." For other ex-slaves, the shock of recognition came upon seeing their parents whipped or upon confronting the fact that their parents were unable to protect them from punishment from a master or an overseer.

For a Virginia slave known only as Charles, the crucial moment came when his white playmates first began to treat him as a slave. His master's son recalled that moment. "It is customary in nearly all households in the South for the white and black children connected with each other to play together," he wrote. "The trial . . . comes when the young Negroes who have hitherto been on this democratic footing with the young whites are presently deserted by their . . . companions, who enter upon school-life . . . ceasing to associate with their swarthy comrades any longer, meet them in the future with the air of the master." Charles responded with bitterness and defiance. He set fire to the family's house and was subsequently sold to the deep South.

16
Jacob Stroyer

"I CANNOT DO ANYTHING FOR YOU"

In the following selection, Jacob Stroyer describes growing up under slavery. Note the ways that some slave children sought to imitate the behavior of their white owners and the ways that slaveowners undermined the authority of slave parents.

Gilbert was a cruel [slave] boy. He used to strip his fellow Negroes while in the woods, and whip them two or three times a week, so that their backs were all scarred, and threatened them with severer punishments if they told; this state of things had been going on for quite a while. As I was a favorite with Gilbert, I always managed to escape a whipping, with the promise of keeping the secret of the punishment of the rest. . . . But finally, one day, Gilbert said to me, "Jake," as he used to call me, "you am a good boy, but I'm gwine to wip you some to-day, as I wip dem toder boys." Of course I was required to strip off my only garment, which was an Osnaburg linen shirt, worn by both sexes of the Negro children in the summer. As I stood trembling before my merciless superior, who had a switch in his hand, thousands of thoughts went through my little mind as to how to get rid of the whipping. I finally fell upon a plan which I hoped would save me from a punishment that was near at hand. . . . I commenced reluctantly to take off my shirt, at the same time pleading with Gilbert, who paid no attention to my prayer. . . . Having satisfied myself that no mercy was to be found with Gilbert, I drew my shirt off and threw it over his head, and bounded forward on a run in the direction of the sound of the [nearby] carpenters. By the time he got from the entanglement of my garment, I had quite a little start of him. . . . As I got near to the carpenters, one of them ran and met me, into whose arms I

Source: Jacob Stroyer, *My Life in the South* (enlarged edition; Salem, Mass., 1898)

jumped. The man into whose arms I ran was Uncle Benjamin, my mother's uncle. . . . I told him that Gilbert had been in the habit of stripping the boys and whipping them two or three times a week, when we went into the woods, and threatened them with greater punishment if they told. . . . Gilbert was brought to trial, severely whipped, and they made him beg all the children to pardon him for his treatment to them.

[My] father . . . used to take care of horses and mules. I was around with him in the barn yard when but a very small boy; of course that gave me an early relish for the occupation of hostler, and I soon made known my preference to Col. Singleton, who was a sportsman, and an owner of fine horses. And, although I was too small to work, the Colonel granted my request; hence I was allowed to be numbered among those who took care of the fine horses and learned to ride. But I soon found that my new occupation demanded a little more than I cared for. It was not long after I had entered my new work before they put me upon the back of a horse which threw me to the ground almost as soon as I had reached his back. It hurt me a little, but that was not the worst of it, for when I got up there was a man standing near with a switch in hand, and he immediately began to beat me. Although I was a very bad boy, this was the first time I had been whipped by anyone except father and mother, so I cried out in a tone of voice as if I would say, this is the first and last whipping you will give me when father gets hold of you.

When I had got away from him I ran to father with all my might, but soon found my expectation blasted, as father very coolly said to me, "Go back to your work and be a good boy, for I cannot do anything for you." But that did not satisfy me, so on I went to mother with my complaint and she came out to the man who had whipped me; he was a groom, a white man master had hired to train the horses. Mother and he began to talk, then he took a whip and started for her, and she ran from him, talking all the time. I ran back and forth between mother and him until he stopped beating her. After the fight between the groom and mother, he took me back to the stable yard and gave me a severe flogging. And, although mother failed to help me at first, still I had faith that when he had taken me back to the stable yard, and commenced whipping me, she would come and stop him, but I looked in vain, for she did not come.

Then the idea first came to me that I, with my dear father and mother and the rest of my fellow Negroes, were doomed to cruel treatment through life, and was defenseless. But when I found that father and mother could not save me from punishment, as they themselves had to submit to the same treatment, I concluded to appeal to the sympathy of the groom, who seemed to have full control over me; but my pitiful cries never touched his sympathy. . . .

One day, about two weeks after Boney Young [the white man who trained horses for Col. Singleton] and mother had the conflict, he called me to him. . . . When I got to him he said, "Go and bring me the switch, sir." I answered, "yes, sir," and off I went and brought him one . . . [and] . . . he gave me a first-class flogging. . . .

When I went home to father and mother, I said to them, "Mr. Young is whipping me too much now, I shall not stand it, I shall fight him." Father said to me, "You must not do that, because if you do he will say that your mother and I advised you to do it, and it will make it hard for your mother and me, as well as for yourself. You must do as I told you, my son: do your work the best you can, and do not say anything." I said to father, "But I don't know what I have done that he should whip me; he does not tell me what wrong I have done, he simply calls me to him and whips me when he gets ready." Father said, "I can do nothing more than to pray to the Lord to hasten the time when these things shall be done away; that is all I can do. . . . "

17
James W.C. Pennington

"THE WANT OF PARENTAL CARE
AND ATTENTION"

In 1849, James W.C. Pennington, the minister of a Presbyterian Church in New York City and the recipient of a degree from the University of Heidelberg in Germany, published a narrative of his life that revealed the astonishing news that he was a fugitive slave and a former blacksmith from Maryland. In his account of his life, Pennington offers the following reflections on the impact of slavery upon slave children.

My feelings are always outraged when I hear [ministers] speak of "kind masters,"—"Christian masters,"—"the mildest form of slavery,"—well fed and clothed slaves," as extenuations of slavery; I am satisfied they either mean to pervert the truth, or they do not know what they say. The being of slavery, its soul and body, lives and moves in the chattel principle, the property principle, the bill of sale principle; the cart-whip, starvation, and nakedness, are its inevitable consequences to a greater or less extent, warring with the dispositions of men. . . .

Another evil of slavery [is] . . . the want of parental care and attention. My parents were not able to give any attention to their children during the day. I often suffered much from hunger and other similar causes. To estimate the sad state of a slave child, you must look at it as a helpless human being thrown upon the world without the benefit of its natural guardians. It is thrown into the world without a social circle to flee to for hope, shelter, comfort, or instruction. The social circle, with all its heaven-ordained bless-

Source: *The Fugitive Blacksmith or, Events in the History of James W.C. Pennington* (2nd ed.; London, 1849)

ings, is of the utmost importance to the tender child; but of this, the slave child, however tender and delicate, is robbed.

There is another source of evil to slave children, which I cannot forbear to mention here, as one which early embittered my life,—I mean the tyranny of the master's children. My master had two sons, about the ages and sizes of my older brother and myself. We were not only required to recognize these young sirs as our young masters, but they felt themselves to be such; and, in consequence of this feeling, they sought to treat us with the same air of authority that their father did the older slaves.

Another evil of slavery that I felt severely about this time, was the tyranny and abuse of the overseers. These men seem to look with an evil eye upon children. I was once visiting a menagerie, and being struck with the fact, that the lion was comparatively indifferent to every one around his cage, while he eyed with peculiar keenness a little boy I had; the keeper informed me that such was always the case. Such is true of those human beings in the slave states, called overseers. They seem to take pleasure in torturing the children of slaves, long before they are large enough to be put at the hoe, and consequently under the whip.

We had an overseer, named Blackstone; he was an extremely cruel man to the working hands. He always carried a long hickory whip, a kind of pole. He kept three or four of these in order, that he might not at any time be without one.

I once found one of these hickories lying in the yard, and supposing that he had thrown it away, I picked it up, and boy-like, was using it for a horse; he came from the field, and seeing me with it, fell upon me with the one he then had in his hand, and flogged me most cruelly. From that, I lived in constant dread of that man; and he would show how much he delighted in cruelty by chasing me from my play with threats and imprecations. I have lain for hours in a wood, or behind a fence, to hide from his eye. . . .

When I was nine years of age, myself and my brother were hired out from home; my brother was placed with a pump-maker, and I was placed with a stone-mason. We were both in a town some six miles from home. As the men with whom we lived were not slaveholders, we enjoyed some relief from the peculiar evils of slavery. Each of us lived in a family where there was no other Negro.

The slaveholders in that state [Maryland] often hire the children of their slaves out to non-slaveholders, not only because they save themselves the expense of taking care of them, but in this way they get among their slaves useful trades. They put a bright slave-boy with a tradesman, until he gets such a knowledge of the trade as to be able to do his own work, and then he takes him home. I remained with the stonemason until I was eleven years of age: at this time I was taken home. This was another serious period in my childhood; I was separated from my older brother, to whom I was much attached; he continued at his place, and not only learned the trade to great perfection, but finally became the property of the man with whom he lived, so that our separation was permanent, as we never lived nearer after, than six miles.

18
Lunsford Lane

"I DISCOVERED THE DIFFERENCE BETWEEN MYSELF AND MY MASTER'S WHITE CHILDREN"

Lunsford Lane, who grew up on a plantation near Raleigh, North Carolina, manufactured pipes and tobacco and succeeded in saving enough money to buy his own freedom and purchase his wife and seven children. Here, he describes his experiences as a slave child.

My father was a slave to a near neighbor. The apartment where I was born and where I spent my childhood and youth was called "the kitchen," situated some fifteen or twenty rods from the "great house." Here the house servants lodged and lived, and here the meals were prepared for the people in the mansion. . . .

My infancy was spent upon the floor, in a rough cradle, or sometimes in my mother's arms. My early boyhood in playing with the other boys and girls, colored and white, in the yard, and occasionally doing such little matters of labor as one of so young years could. I knew no difference between myself and the white children; nor did they seem to know any in turn. Sometimes my master would come out and give a biscuit to me, and another to one of his own white boys; but I did not perceive the difference between us. I had no brothers or sisters, but there were other colored families living in the same kitchen, and the children played in the same yard with me and my mother. . . .

When I began to work, I discovered the difference between myself and my master's white children. They began to order me about, and were told to do so by my master and mistress. I found, too, that they had learned to read, while I was not permitted to have a book in my hand. To be in possession of anything written or printed, was regarded as an offence. And then there was the fear

Source: *The Narrative of Lunsford Lane* (Boston, 1842).

that I might be sold away from those who were dear to me, and conveyed to the far South. I had learned that being a slave I was subject to the worst (to us) of all calamities; and I knew of others in similar situations to myself, thus sold away. My friends were not numerous; but in proportion as they were few they were dear; and the thought that I might be separated from them forever, was like that of having the heart wrenched from its socket; while the idea of being conveyed to the far South, seemed infinitely worse than the terrors of death.

Part 6

FAMILY:

"Nobody Knows de Trouble I See"

A former slave reacted bitterly to the remark that his former master had been kind to his slaves. "Kind! I was dat man's slave; and he sold my wife, and he sold my two chill'en ... Kind!, yes, he gib me corn enough, and he gib me pork enough, and he neber gib me one lick wid de whip, but whar's my wife?—whar's my chill'en? Take away de pork, I say; take away de corn, I can work and raise dese for myself; but gib me back de wife of my bosom, and gib me back my poor chill'en as was sold away."

Nothing provided greater ammunition for critics of slavery than the outrages committed on slave families. Southern law did not recognize or protect slave marriages or slave family ties. Slaveowners were free to sell husbands from wives and parents from children and sexually to exploit slave wives or daughters.

Certainly, many owners believed that it was in their own self-interest to encourage stable family lives. They knew that stable families raised slave morale, reduced the likelihood of slaves running away, and encouraged a high slave birth rate. Thus, many slaveholders promoted stable families by participating in slave marriage ceremonies, providing slave families with separate garden plots, prohibiting divorce, and severely punishing adultery.

But slaveowners also regarded slaves as a form of property that might be sold at any time. In conducting marriages, slaveholders pointedly omitted any words that indicated that slave unions were perpetual. A former slave noted that masters would never say " 'What God done jined, cain't no man pull asunder.' " Instead, they "jus' say, 'Now you married." A slave preacher thought slaveowners should conclude the ceremony with the words: "till death or buckra [master] do you part."

Many slave spouses resided on separate farms or plantations. Millie Barber's parents lived five miles apart, and her father could only visit his family if he received permission from his owner. As she later recalled: "My pa have to git a pass to come to see my mammy. He come sometimes widout de pass. Patrollers catch him way up de chimney hidin' one night; they stripped him right befo' mammy and give him thirty-nine lashes." After purchasing new slaves, some masters required them to take new husbands or wives. A former Louisiana slave, Stephen Jordon, described the anguish that this could cause: "I myself had my wife on another plantation. The woman my master gave me had a husband on another plantation. Every thing was mixed up. My other wife had two children for me, but the woman master gave me had no children. We were put in the same cabin, but both of us cried, me for my old wife and she for her old husband."

Despite the possibility of disruption, slaves were intensely committed to their families. To perpetuate a sense of family identity, slave parents named their children after ancestors or relatives. The strength of slave family ties is also suggested by the number of advertisements for runaway slaves that indicate that the fugitives were seeking to visit family members who lived on separate plantations.

Surviving slave letters provide a graphic record of the strength of slave families. After learning that he was going to be sold away from his family, a slave named Abream Scriven wrote to his wife: "My dear wife for you and my Children my pen cannot Express the griffe I feel to parted from you all.... I remain your truly husband until Death." A Tennessee slave named George Pleasant, expressed similar sentiments to his wife, who lived in North Carolina: "I hope with God's helpe that I may be abble to rejoys with you on the earth and In heaven lets meet when [God] will."

19
Laura Spicer

"IT NEVER WAS OUR WISH TO BE SEPARATED"

When he and his wife were sold apart, Laura Spicer's husband remarried, thinking that he would never see her again. After the Civil War, however, Laura found him, prompting anguish and confusion.

I don't know whether I have told you Laura Spicer's story. She was sold from her husband some years ago, and he, hearing she was dead, married again. He has had a wavering inclination to again unite his fortunes with hers; and she has received a letter from him in which he said, "I read you letters over and over again. I keep them always in my pocket. If you are married I don't ever want to see you again." And yet, in some of his letters, he says, "I would much rather you would get married to some good man, for every time I gits a letter from you it tears me all to pieces. The reason why I have not written you before, in a long time, is because your letters disturbed me so very much. You know I love my children. I treats them good as a Father can treat his children; and I do a good deal of it for you. I was sorry to hear that Lewellyn, my poor little son, have had such bad health. I would come and see you, but I know you could not bear it. I want to see you and I don't want to see you. I love you just as well as I did the last day I saw you, and it will not do for you and I to meet. I am married, and my wife have two children, and if you and I meets it would make a very dissatisfied family."

Some of the children are with the mother and the father writes, "Send me some of the children's hair in a separate paper with their names on the paper. Will you please git married, as long as I am married. My dear, you know the Lord know both of our

Source: Unsigned and undated letter (1869?) in the Chase Papers, American Antiquarian Society, Worcester, Massachusetts.

hearts. You know it never was our wishes to be separated from each other, and it never was our fault. Oh, I can see you so plain, at any-time, I had rather anything to have happened to me most than ever have been parted from you and the children. As I am, I do not know which I love best, you or Anna. If I was to die, today or tomorrow, I do not think I would die satisfied till you tell me you will try and marry some good, smart man that will take good care of you and the children; and do it because you love me; and not because I think more of the wife I have got than I do of you. The woman is not born that feels as near to me as you do. You feel this day like myself. Tell them [the children] they must remember they have a good father and one that cares for them and one that thinks about them every day. —My heart did ache when reading your very kind and interesting letter. Laura I do not think that I have changed any at all since I saw you last—I thinks of you and my children every day of my life. Laura I do love you the same. My love to you never have failed. Laura, truly, I have got another wife, and I am very sorry, that I am. You feels and seems to me as much like my dear loving wife, as you ever did Laura."

20
Josiah Henson

"THE OVERSEER ... SENT MY MOTHER AWAY ... TO A RETIRED SPOT"

Nothing aroused greater fury within the slave community than the sexual abuse of slave women. Josiah Henson describes his father's reaction to an overseer's attempt to molest his mother.

I was born June 15th, 1789, in Charles County, Maryland, on a farm belonging to Mr. Francis Newman, about a mile from Port Tobacco. My mother was a slave of Dr. Josiah McPherson, but hired to the Mr. Newman to whom my father belonged. The only incident I can remember which occurred while my mother continued on Mr. Newman's farm, was the appearance one day of my father with his head bloody and his back lacerated. He was beside himself with mingled rage and suffering. The explanation I picked up from the conversation of others only partially explained the matter to my mind; but as I grew older I understood it all. It seemed the overseer had sent my mother away from the other field hands to a retired place, and after trying persuasion in vain, had resorted to force to accomplish a brutal purpose. Her screams aroused my father at his distant work, and running up, he found his wife struggling with the man. Furious at the sight, he sprung upon him like a tiger. In a moment the overseer was down, and, mastered by rage, my father would have killed him but for the entreaties of my mother, and the overseer's own promise that nothing should ever be said of the matter. The promise was kept—like most promises of the cowardly and debased—as long as the danger lasted.

The laws of state provide means and opportunities for

Source: Josiah Henson, *Uncle Tom's Story of His Life: An Autobiography of the Rev. Josiah Henson* (London, 1877).

revenge so ample, that miscreants like him never fail to improve them. "A nigger has struck a white man;" that is enough to set a whole county on fire; no question is asked about the provocation. The authorities were soon in pursuit of my father. The fact of the sacrilegious act of lifting a hand against the sacred temple of a white man's body . . . this was all it was necessary to establish. And the penalty followed: one hundred lashes on the bare back, and to have the right ear nailed to the whipping-post, and then severed from the body. For a time my father kept out of the way, hiding in the woods, and at night venturing into some cabin in search of food. But at length the strict watch set baffled all his efforts. His supplies cut off, he was fairly starved out, and compelled by hunger to come back and give himself up.

The day for the execution of the penalty was appointed. The Negroes from the neighboring plantations were summoned, for their moral improvement, to witness the scene. A powerful blacksmith named Hewes laid on the stripes. Fifty were given, during which the cries of my father might be heard a mile, and then a pause ensued. True, he had struck a white man, but as valuable property he must not be damaged. Judicious men felt his pulse. Oh! he could stand the whole. Again and again the thong fell on his lacerated back. His cries grew fainter and fainter, till a feeble groan was the only response to his final blows. His head was then thrust against the post, and his right ear fastened to it with a tack; a swift pass of a knife, and the bleeding member was left sticking to the place. Then came a hurrah from the degraded crowd, and the exclamation, "That's what he's got for striking a white man." A few said, "it's a damned shame;" but the majority regarded it as but a proper tribute to their offended majesty. . . .

Previous to this affair my father, from all I can learn, had been a good-humored and light-hearted man, the ringleader in all fun at corn-huskings and Christmas buffoonery. His banjo was the life of the farm, and all night long at a merry-making would he play on it while the other Negroes danced. But from this hour he became utterly changed. Sullen, morose, and dogged, nothing could be done with him. The milk of human kindness in his heart was turned to gall. He brooded over his wrongs. No fear or threats of being sold to the far south—the greatest of all terrors to the Maryland slave—would render him tractable. So off he was sent to Alabama. What was his fate neither my mother nor I have ever learned. . . .

For two or three years my mother and her young family of six children had resided on [Dr. McPherson's] estate; and we had been in the main very happy. . . .

Our term of happy union as one family was now, alas! at an end. Mournful as was the Doctor's death to his friends it was a far greater calamity to us. The estate and the slaves must be sold and the proceeds divided among the heirs. We were but property—not a mother, and the children God had given her.

Common as are slave-auctions in the Southern states, and naturally as a slave may look forward to the time when he will be put upon the block, still the full misery of the event—of the scenes which precede and succeed it—is never understood till the actual experience comes. The first sad announcement that the sale is to be; the knowledge that all ties of the past are to be sundered; the frantic terror at the idea of being "sent South;" the almost certainty that one member of a family will be torn from another; the anxious scanning of purchasers' faces; the agony at parting, often forever, with husband, wife, child—these must be seen and felt to be fully understood. Young as I was then, the iron entered into my soul. The remembrance of breaking up of McPherson's estate is photographed in its minutest features in my mind. The crowd collected around the stand, the huddling group of Negroes, the examination of muscle, teeth, the exhibition of agility, the look of the autioneer, the agony of my mother—I can shut my eyes and see them all.

My brothers and sisters were bid off first, and one by one, while my mother, paralyzed by grief, held me by the hand. Her turn came, and she was bought by Isaac Riley of Montgomery County. Then I was offered to the assembled purchasers. My mother, half distracted by the thought of parting forever from all her children, pushed through the crowd, while the bidding for me was going on, to the spot where Riley was standing. She fell at his feet and clung to his knees, entreating him in tones that a mother only could command, to buy her baby as well as herself, and spare to her one, at least of her little ones. Will it, can it be believed that this man, thus appealed to, was capable not merely of turning a deaf ear to her supplication, but of disengaging himself from her with such violent blows and kicks, as to reduce her to the necessity of creeping out of his reach, and mingling the groan of bodily suffering with the sob of a breaking heart? As she crawled away from the brutal man I heard her sob out, "Oh, Lord Jesus, how long, how long shall I suffer this way!" I must have been then between five and six years old. I seem to see and hear my poor weeping mother now. This was one of my earliest observations of men; an experience which I only shared with thousands of my race, the bitterness of which to any individual who suffers it cannot be diminished by the frequency of its recurrence, while it is dark enough to overshadow the whole after-life with something blacker than a funeral pall.

21
Lewis Clarke

"THERE IS BUT ... LITTLE SCRUPLE OF SEPARATING FAMILIES"

Lewis Clarke, the son of a Scottish weaver and a slave mother, was born in Kentucky in 1815. Despite an agreement that she was to be freed upon her husband's death, Clarke's mother and her nine children remained in slavery. After he learned that he was going to be sold in New Orleans, Clarke successfully fled through Ohio across Lake Erie to Canada in 1841. In an account of his life published in 1846, he provided answers to questions he was frequently asked about the impact of slavery upon slave families.

[Question] Are families often separated? How many such cases have you personally known?

[Answer]—I never knew a whole family to live together till all were grown up in my life. There is almost always, in every family, some one or more keen and bright, or else sullen and stubborn slave, whose influence they are afraid of on the rest of the family, and such a one must take a walking ticket to the South.

There are other causes of separation. The death of a large owner is the occasion usually of many families being broken up. Bankruptcy is another cause of separation, and the hard-heartedness of a majority of slave-holders another and a more fruitful cause than either or all the rest. Generally there is but little more scruple about separating families than there is with a man who keeps sheep in selling off the lambs in the fall. On one plantation where I lived, there was an old slave named Paris. He was from

Source: *Interesting Memoirs and Documents Relating to American Slavery, and the Glorious Struggle Now Making for Complete Emancipation* (London, 1846).

fifty to sixty years old, and a very honest and apparently pious slave. A slave-trader came along one day, to gather hands for the South. The old master ordered the waiter or coachman to take Paris into the back room pluck out all his gray hairs, rub his face with a greasy towel, and then had him brought forward and sold for a young man. His wife consented to go with him, upon a promise from the trader that they should be sold together, with their youngest child, which she carried in her arms. They left two behind them, who were only from four to six or eight years of age. The speculator collected his drove, started for the market, and, before he left the state, he sold that infant child to pay one of his tavern bills, and took the balance in cash. . . .

[Question] Have you ever known a slave mother to kill her own children?

[Answer] There was a slave mother near where I lived, who took her child into the cellar and killed it. She did it to prevent being separated from her child. Another slave mother took her three children and threw them into a well, and then jumped in with them, and they were all drowned. Other instances I have frequently heard of. At the death of many and many a slave child, I have seen the two feelings struggling in the bosom of a mother—joy, that it was beyond the reach of the slave monsters, and the natural grief of a mother over her child. In the presence of the master, grief seems to predominate; when away from them, they rejoice that there is one whom the slave-killer will never torment.

Part 7

RELIGION:

"Go Home to My Lord and Be Free"

Some slaveholders were quite open in their belief that religion could serve as a valuable mechanism of social control, instilling submissiveness and conscientiousness within slaves. One 1845 pamphlet asserted that Christianity could promote "good will," "meekness," "patience," "truth and faithfulness." But Christian religion also had another face, emphasizing judgment, equality, and liberation. As one white observer in Georgia commented, the slaves believe "that in the life to come there will also be white people and black people; but then the white people will be slaves, and they shall have the dominion over them."

During the seventeenth century, slaveowners were reluctant to Christianize their slaves for fear that baptized slaves would have to be set free. They also worried that the Christian notion of the spiritual equality of all human beings would lead slaves to demand their freedom. Many slaves rejected Christianity because, as one white observer put it, a "Fondness they have for their old Heathenish Rites, and the strong Prejudice they must have against Teachers from among those, whom they serve so unwillingly."

By the second quarter of the eighteenth century, a growing number of slaveholders concluded that Christianity would make slaves more docile and conscientious, by placing them "under strong Obligations to perform [their] duties with the greatest Diligence and Fidelity . . . from a Sense of Duty to God, and the Belief and Expectation of a future account." The process of converting slaves to Christianity began in earnest during the Great Awakening of the 1730s and 1740s and then accelerated in the late eighteenth century.

Within the Baptist and Methodist churches, slaves began to cre-

105

ate a hybrid African-American form of Christianity, blending Christian rituals and beliefs with elements of West African culture. The result, as Albert J. Raboteau has shown, was a religion with its own distinctive forms of preaching and worship, characterized by rhythmic sermons, "shouting" and other ecstatic behavior induced by spiritual possession, and forms of singing and dancing influenced by slaves' African traditions.

On individual plantations, slaves held informal or secret prayer meetings, apart from the influence of their masters. Here slave preachers conducted baptisms, weddings, and funerals, and slaves sang spirituals, which blended Christian hymns and psalms with African styles and gave expression to the slaves' intense desire for freedom and transcendence. Slave religion, in turn, co-existed alongside folk traditions with African roots, like witchcraft, herbalism, and conjure (which involved supernatural spells and charms) that addressed needs unmet by Protestant Christianity.

22
Olaudah Equiano

"THE STRONG ANALOGY ... IN THE MANNERS ... OF MY COUNTRYMEN, AND THOSE OF THE JEWS"

Religion played a central role in the cultures of West Africa. In this extract from his memoirs, Olaudah Equiano describes Ibo religion in Eastern Nigeria and observes that certain aspects of African religious belief resemble those found in Judaism and Christianity.

As to religion, the natives believe that there is one Creator of all things, and that he lives in the sun, and is girded round with a belt, that he may never eat or drink; but according to some, he smokes a pipe, which is our own favorite luxury. They believe he governs events, especially our deaths or captivity; but, as for the doctrine of eternity, I do not remember to have ever heard of it: some however believe in the transmigration of souls in a certain degree. Those spirits, which are not transmigrated, such as their dear friends or relations, they believe always attend them, and guard them from the bad spirits of their foes. For this reason, they always, before eating, as I have observed, put some small portion of the meat, and pour some of their drink, on the ground for them; and they often make oblations of the blood of beasts or fowls at their graves. I was very fond of my mother, and almost constantly with her. When she went to make these oblations at her mother's tomb, which was a kind of small solitary thatched house, I sometimes attended her. There she made her libations, and spent most of the night in cries and lamentation....

We compute the year from the day on which the sun crosses the line; and, on its setting that evening, there is a general shout

Source: *The Interesting Narrative of the Life of Olaudah Equiano or Gustavus Vassa the African* (London, 1789).

throughout the land; at least, I can speak from my own knowledge, throughout our vicinity. The people at the same time made a great noise with rattles not unlike the basket rattles used by children here, though much larger, and hold up their hands to heaven for a blessing. It is then the greatest offerings are made; and those children whom our wise men foretell will be fortunate are then presented to different people. . . . They have many offerings, particularly at full moons, generally two at harvest, before the fruits are taken out of the ground; and, when any young animals are killed, sometimes they offer up part of them as a sacrifice. . . .

We practiced circumcision like the Jews, and made offerings and feasts on that occasion in the same manner as they did. Like them also our children were named from some event, some circumstance, or fancied foreboding, at the time of their birth. I was named Olaudah, which, in our language, signifies vicissitude, or fortune also; one favored, and having a loud voice, and well spoken. I remember we never polluted the name of the object of our adoration; on the contrary, it was always mentioned with the greatest reverence; and we were totally unacquainted with swearing, and all those terms of abuse and reproach which find their way so readily and copiously into the language of more civilized people. The only expressions of that kind I remember were "May you rot, or may you swell, or may a beast take you."

I have before remarked, that the natives of this part of Africa are extremely cleanly. This necessary habit of decency was with us a part of religion, and therefore we had many purifications and washings. . . . Those that touched the dead at any time were obliged to wash and purify themselves before they could enter a dwelling house. Every woman too, at certain times, was forbidden to come into a dwelling-house, or touch any person, or anything we eat. I was so fond of my mother I could not keep from her, or avoid touching her at some of those periods, in consequence of which I was obliged to be kept out with her in a little house made for that purpose, till offering was made, and then we were purified.

Though we had no places of public worship, we had priests and magicians, or wise men. I do not remember whether they had different offices, or whether they were united in the same persons, but they were held in great reverence by the people. They calculated our time and foretold events. . . . They wore their beards; and, when they died, they were succeeded by their sons. Most of their implements and things of value were interred along with them. Pipes and tobacco were also put into the grave with the corpse, which was always perfumed and ornamented; and animals were offered in sacrifice to them. None accompanied their funerals, but those of the same profession or tribe. These buried them after sunset, and always returned from the grave by a different way from that which they went.

These magicians were also our doctors or physicians. They practiced bleeding by cupping; and were very successful in healing wounds and expelling poisons. They had likewise some extraordinary method of discovering jealousy, theft, and poisoning; the success of which no doubt they derived from the unbounded influence over the credulity and superstition of the people. I do not remember what those methods were, except that as to poisoning. I recollect an instance or two, which I hope it will not be deemed impertinent here to insert, as it may serve as a kind of specimen of the rest, and is still used by the Negroes in the West Indies. A young woman had been poisoned, but it was not known by whom: the doctor ordered the corpse to be taken up by some persons, and carried to the grave. As soon as the bearers had raised it on their shoulders, they seemed seized with some sudden impulse, and ran to and fro, unable to stop themselves. At last, after having passed through a number of thorns and prickly bushes unhurt, the corpse fell from them close to a house, and defaced it in the fall; and the owner being taken up, he immediately confessed the poisoning. . . .

Such is the imperfect sketch my memory has furnished me of the manner and customs of a people among whom I first drew my breath. And here I cannot forbear suggesting what has long struck me very forcibly, namely, the strong analogy which even by this sketch, imperfect as it is, appears to prevail in the manners and customs of my countrymen, and those of the Jews, before they reached the Land of Promise. . . . Like the Israelites in their primitive state, our government was conducted by our chiefs, our judges, our wise men, and elders; and the head of a family with us enjoyed a similar authority over his household with that which is ascribed to Abraham and the other patriarchs. The law of retaliation obtained almost universally with us as with them: and even their religion appeared to have shed upon us a ray of its glory, though broken and spent in its passage, or eclipsed by the cloud with which time, tradition, and ignorance, might have enveloped it: for we had our circumcision (a rule I believe peculiar to that people): we had also our sacrifices and burnt-offerings, our washings and purifications, on the same occasions as they had.

23
Charles Ball

"I ASSISTED . . . TO INTER THE INFANT"

*During the early nineteenth century, some slaves continued
to draw upon West African religious customs in burying
the dead. In this selection, Charles Ball, a slave in Western
Maryland, describes a slave funeral:*

I assisted her and her husband to inter the infant . . . and its
father buried with it, a small bow and several arrows; a little bag
of parched meal; a miniature canoe, about a foot long, and a little
paddle, (with which he said it would cross the ocean to his own
country) a small stick, with an iron nail, sharpened and fastened
into one end of it; and a piece of white muslin, with several curi-
ous and strange figures painted on it in blue and red, by which, he
said, his relations and countrymen would know the infant to be his
son, and would receive it accordingly, on its arrival amongst them
. . . He cut a lock of hair from his head, threw it upon the dead
infant, and closed the grave with his own hands. He then told us
the God of his country was looking at him, and was pleased with
what he had done.

Source: Charles Ball, *Slavery in the United States: A Narrative of the Life and Adventures of Charles Ball, A Black Man* (New York, 1837).

24
Peter Randolph

"THE SLAVES ASSEMBLE IN
THE SWAMPS"

Peter Randolph, who grew up in slavery on a plantation in Prince George County, Virginia, received his freedom in 1847 following his owner's death, and then served as an antislavery agent, a newspaper editor, and as a Baptist minister in the North and in Canada. Following the Civil War, he served as minister in the Ryland or Old African Baptist Church in Richmond, Virginia. This selection describes the disparity between the version of Christianity that masters taught to the slaves and the version that slaves taught to themselves.

Many say the Negroes receive religious education—that Sabbath worship is instituted for them as for others, and were it not for slavery, they would die in their sins—that really, the institution of slavery is a benevolent missionary enterprise. Yes, they are preached to, and I will give my readers some faint glimpses of these preachers, and their doctrines and practices.

In Prince George County there were two meeting-houses intended for public worship. Both were occupied by the Baptist denomination. These houses were built by William and George Harrison, brothers . . . that their slaves might go there on the Sabbath and receive instruction, such as slave-holding ministers would give. The prominent preaching to the slaves was, " 'Servants, obey your masters'. Do not steal or lie, for this is very wrong. Such conduct is sinning against the Holy Ghost, and is base ingratitude to your kind masters, who feed, clothe and protect you. . . . " I should think, when making such statements, the slaveholders would feel the rebuke of the Apostle and fall down and be carried

Source: Peter Randolph, *Slave Cabin to the Pulpit* (Boston, 1893).

out from the face of day, as were Ananias and Sapphira, when they betrayed the trust committed to them, or refused to bear true testimony in regard to that trust.

There was another church, about fourteen miles from the one just mentioned. It was called "Brandon's church", and there the white Baptists worshiped. . . .

There was one Brother Shell who used to preach. One Sabbath, while exhorting the poor, impenitent, hard-hearted, ungrateful slaves, so much beloved by their masters, to repentance and prayerfulness, while entreating them to lead good lives, that they might escape the wrath (of the lash) to come, some of his crocodile tears overflowed his cheek. . . . But, my readers, Monday morning, Brother Shell was afflicted with his old malady, hardness of heart, so that he was obliged to catch one of the sisters by the throat, and give her a terrible flogging.

The like of this is the preaching, and these are the men that spread the Gospel among the slaves. Ah! such a Gospel had better be buried in oblivion, for it makes more heathens than Christians. Such preachers ought to be forbidden by the laws of the land ever to mock again at the blessed religion of Jesus, which was sent as a light to the world. . . .

Not being allowed to hold meetings on the plantation, the slaves assemble in the swamps, out of reach of the patrols. They have an understanding among themselves as to the time and place of getting together. This is often done by the first one arriving breaking boughs from the trees, and bending them in the direction of the selected spot. Arrangements are then made for conducting the exercises. They first ask each other how they feel, the state of their minds, etc. The male members then select a certain space, in separate groups, for their division of the meeting. Preaching in order, by the brethren; then praying and singing all round, until they generally feel quite happy. The speaker usually commences by calling himself unworthy, and talks very slowly, until, feeling the spirit, he grows excited, and in a short time, there fall to the ground twenty or thirty men and women under its influence. Enlightened people call it excitement; but I wish the same was felt by everybody, so far as they are sincere.

The slave forgets all his sufferings, except to remind others of the trials during the past week, exclaiming: "Thank God, I shall not live here always!" Then they pass from one to another, shaking hands, and bidding each other farewell, promising, should they meet no more on earth, to strive and meet in heaven, where all is

joy, happiness and liberty. As they separate, they sing a parting
hymn of praise.

Sometimes the slaves meet in an old log-cabin, when they
find it necessary to keep a watch. If discovered, they escape, if possible; but those who are caught often get whipped. Some are willing to be punished thus for Jesus' sake. Most of the songs used in
worship are composed by the slaves themselves, and describe their
own sufferings. Thus:

> "Oh, that I had a bosom friend,
> To tell my secrets to,
> One always to depend upon
> In everything I do!"

> "How do I wander, up and down!
> I seem a stranger, quite undone;
> None to lend an ear to my complaint,
> No one to cheer me, though I faint."

Some of the slaves sing—

> "No more rain, no more snow,
> No more cowskin on my back!"

Then they change it by singing—

> "Glory be to God that rules on high."

In some places, if the slaves are caught praying to God, they
are whipped more than if they had committed a great crime. The
slaveholders will allow the slaves to dance, but do not want them
to pray to God. Sometimes, when a slave, on being whipped, calls
upon God, he is forbidden to do so, under threat of having his
throat cut, or brains blown out. Oh, reader! this seems very hard—
that slaves cannot call on their Maker, when the case most needs it.
Sometimes the poor slave takes courage to ask his master to let
him pray, and is driven away, with the answer, that if discovered
praying, his back will pay the bill.

25

Henry Bibb

"MANY BELIEVE ... IN WHAT THEY CALL CONJURATION"

Henry Bibb, born to a white father and a slave mother in Shelby County, Kentucky, in 1815, was held in slavery in Kentucky, Louisiana, and in present-day Arkansas. In 1837, he escaped through Ohio and Michigan into Canada. In this selection, he describes slaves' notions of conjure that existed alongside Christianity.

In 1833, I had some very serious religious impressions, and there was quite a number of slaves in that neighborhood, who felt very desirous to be taught to read the Bible. There was a Miss Davis, a poor white girl, who offered to teach a Sabbath School for the slaves, notwithstanding public opinion and the law was opposed to it. Books were furnished and she commenced the school; but the news soon got to our owners that she was teaching us to read. This caused quite an excitement in the neighborhood. Patrols were appointed to go and break it up the next Sabbath. They were determined that we should not have a Sabbath School in operation. For slaves this was called an incendiary movement.

The Sabbath is not regarded by a large number of the slaves as a day of rest. They have no schools to go to; no moral nor religious instruction at all in many localities where there are hundreds of slaves. Hence they resort to some kind of amusement. Those who make no profession of religion, resort to the woods in large numbers on that day to gamble, fight, get drunk, and break the Sabbath. This is often encouraged by slaveholders. When they wish to have a little sport of that kind, they go among the slaves

Source: *Narrative of the Life and Adventures of Henry Bibb, An American Slave* (New York, 1849).

and give them whiskey, to see them dance, "pat juber," sing and play on the banjo. Then get them to wrestling, fighting, jumping, running foot races, and butting each other like sheep. This is urged on by giving them whiskey; making bets on them; laying chips on one slave's head, and daring another to tip it off with his hand; and if he tipped it off, it would be called an insult, and cause a fight. Before fighting, the parties choose their seconds to stand by them while fighting; a ring or a circle is formed to fight in, and no one is allowed to enter the ring while they are fighting, but their seconds, and the white gentlemen. They are not allowed to fight a duel, nor to use weapons of any kind. The blows are made by kicking, knocking, and butting with their heads; they grab each other by their ears, and jam their heads together like sheep. If they are likely to hurt each other very bad, their masters would rap them with their walking canes, and make them stop. After fighting they make friends, shake hands, and take a dram together, and there is no more of it.

But this is all principally for want of moral instruction. This is where they have no Sabbath Schools; no one to read the Bible to them; no one to preach the gospel who is competent to expound the Scriptures, except slaveholders. And the slaves, with but few exceptions, have no confidence at all in their preaching, because they preach a pro-slavery doctrine. They say, "Servants be obedient to your masters;—and he that knoweth his master's will and doeth it not, shall be beaten, with many stripes;—" means that God will send them to hell, if they disobey their masters. This kind of preaching has driven thousands into infidelity. They view themselves as suffering unjustly under the lash, without friends, without protection of law or gospel, and the green-eyed monster tyranny staring them in the face. They know that they are destined to die in that wretched condition, unless they are delivered by the arm of Omnipotence. And they cannot believe or trust in such a religion, as above named. . . .

There is much superstition among the slaves. Many of them believe in what they call "conjuration," tricking, and witchcraft; and some of them pretend to understand the art, and say that by it they can prevent their masters from exercising their will over their slaves. Such are often applied to by others, to give them power to prevent their masters from flogging them. The remedy is most generally some kind of bitter root; they are directed to chew it and spit towards their masters when they are angry with the slaves. At other times they prepare certain kinds of powders, to sprinkle about their master's dwellings. This is all done for the purpose of defending themselves in some peaceable manner, although I am satisfied that there is no virtue at all in it. . . .

[A conjurer] said if I would pay him a small sum, he would prevent my being flogged. After I had paid him, he mixed up some alum, salt and other stuff into a powder, and said I must sprinkle it about my master, if he should offer to strike me; this would prevent him. He also gave me some kind of bitter root to chew, and spit towards him, which would certainly prevent my being flogged. According to order I used his remedy, and for some cause I was let pass without being flogged that time.

I had then great faith in conjuration and witchcraft. I was led to believe that I could do almost as I pleased, without being flogged. So on the next Sabbath my conjuration was fully tested by my going off, and staying away until Monday morning, without permission. When I returned home, my master declared that he would punish me for going off; but I did not believe that he could do it, while I had this root and dust; and as he approached me, I commenced talking saucy to him. But he soon convinced me that there was no virtue in them. He became so enraged at me for saucing him, that he grasped a handful of switches and punished me severely, in spite of all my roots and powders. . . .

I wanted to be well thought of by [young women], and would go to great lengths to gain their affection. I had been taught by the old superstitious slaves, to believe in conjuration, and it was hard for me to give up the notion, for all I had been deceived by them. One of these conjurers, for a small sum, agreed to teach me to make any girl love me that I wished. After I had paid him, he told me to get a bull frog, and take a certain bone out of the frog, dry it, and when I got a chance I must step up to any girl whom I wished to make love me, and scratch her somewhere on her naked skin with this bone, and she would be certain to love me, and would follow me in spite of herself; no matter who she might be engaged to, nor who she might be walking with.

So I got me a bone for a certain girl, whom I knew to be under the influence of another young man. I happened to meet her in the company of her lover, one Sunday evening, walking out; so when I got a chance, I fetched her a tremendous rasp across her neck with this bone, which made her jump. But in place of making her love me, it only made her angry with me. She felt more like running after me to retaliate on me for thus abusing her, than she felt like loving me.

Part 8

PUNISHMENT:

"Oppressed So Hard They Could Not Stand"

Dr. John Wesley Monette, an apologist for slavery, rejected the charge that whipping slaves was cruel and barbaric. He acknowledged that to anyone unacquainted with the lash, "hearing the loud sharp crack of the whip upon the naked skin, would almost tremble for the life of the poor sufferer." But, he assured his readers, there was no reason for anxiety. "After hearing fifty or one hundred stripes thus being laid on," one would "find the skin not broken, and not a drop of blood drawn from him!" Indeed, he insisted, a buckskin whip's end was so soft that one "could scarcely hurt a child with it." He acknowledged that a lashing "stings, or 'burns' the skin smartly," but, he added, it "does not bruise it." Though slaveowners tried to disguise this fact, they relied on physical punishment to force slaves to toil for long hours and meager rewards.

Though slaveowners, like Monette, tried to deny—or obscure— the cruelty of slavery, the fact remains that slave management was based on fear.

A Georgia slaveowner maintained that "the surest and best method of managing Negroes, is to love them." "If we love our horse . . . he will become gentle, docile and obedient," he observed. "Why will it not have the same effect upon slaves." Many slaveholders offered a variety of rewards and incentives; they gave slaves small garden patches on which they could raise their own crops, distributed gifts, and offered cash bonuses and special holidays to particularly diligent slaves. A few masters actually made profit-sharing agreements with slaves.

Yet even the most humane masters balanced the hope of reward with the threat of punishment. A slaveowner might deny disobedient

*or unproductive slaves passes off of the plantation or reduce their
rations. One Maryland planter forced a slave to eat worms that she
had failed to pick off of a tobacco plant. One farmer described his
approach to discipline: "I do not punish often, but I seldom let an
offense pass." He disciplined children by "pulling an ear, or a sound
box." He placed adults in solitary confinement within a windowless
"hewed log house, with a good substantial door, lock and key."*

*Ultimately a master's authority rested on the threat of physical
pain. To discipline slaves, plantation owners set up private jails, confined slaves in stocks, and shackled them with chains and iron collars.
It was the whip, however, that became the defining symbol of slavery.
A Louisiana planter declared that "the highest punishment must not
exceed 100 lashes in one day and to that extent only in extreme cases.
In general 15 to 20 lashes will be a sufficient flogging."*

26
Frederick Douglass

"MATTERS FOR WHICH A SLAVE MAY BE WHIPPED"

Perhaps the nineteenth century's staunchest advocate of equal rights, Frederick Douglass was born into slavery on Maryland's Eastern shore in 1818, the son of a slave woman and an unknown white man. While toiling as a ship's caulker, he taught himself to read. After he escaped from slavery at the age of twenty, he became the abolitionist movement's most effective orator and published an influential anti-slavery newspaper, The North Star. *In this excerpt from one of his three autobiographies, he describes the circumstances that prompted slaveowners to whip slaves.*

A mere look, word, or motion,—a mistake, accident, or want of power,—are all matters for which a slave may be whipped at any time. Does a slave look dissatisfied? It is said, he has the devil in him, and it must be whipped out. Does he speak loudly when spoken to by his master? Then he is getting high-minded, and should be taken down a button-hole lower. Does he forget to pull off his hat at the approach of a white person? Then he is wanting in reverence, and should be whipped for it. Does he ever venture to vindicate his conduct, when censured for it? Then he is guilty of impudence,—one of the greatest crimes of which a slave can be guilty. Does he ever venture to suggest a different mode of doing things from that pointed out by his master? He is indeed presumptuous, and getting above himself. . . .

Source: *Narrative of the Life of Frederick Douglass, An American Slave* (3rd. English ed., Leeds, 1846)

27
John Brown

"FIXED BELLS AND HORNS ON MY HEAD"

John Brown, who was born into slavery in Southampton County, Virginia, and later toiled in Georgia and Louisiana, describes the methods of discipline employed by one of his owners.

To prevent my running any more, Stevens fixed bells and horns on my head. This is not by any means an uncommon punishment. I have seen many slaves wearing them. A circle of iron, having a hinge behind, with a staple and padlock before, which hang under the chin, is fastened round the neck. Another circle of iron fits quite close round the crown of the head. The two are held together in this position by three rods of iron, which are fixed in each circle. These rods, or horns, stick out three feet above the head, and have a bell attached to each. The bells and horns do not weigh less than twelve to fourteen pounds. When Stevens had fixed this ornament on my head, he turned me loose, and told me I might run off now if I liked.

I wore the bells and horns, day and night, for three months, and I do not think any description I could give of my sufferings during this time would convey anything approaching to a faint idea of them. Let alone that their weight made my head and neck ache dreadfully, especially when I stooped to my work. At night I could not lie down to rest, because the horns prevented my stretching myself, or even curling myself up; so I was obliged to sleep crouching. Of course it was impossible for me to attempt to remove them, or to get away, though I still held to my resolution to make another venture as soon as I could see my way of doing it.

Source: John Brown, *Slave Life in Georgia: A Narrative of the Life, Sufferings, and Escape of John Brown, A Fugitive Slave, Now in England* (London, 1855).

28
William Wells Brown

"I WAS TIED UP IN THE SMOKEHOUSE"

One of the nation's first black novelists and historians, William Wells Brown was born in Lexington, Kentucky, in 1816 and raised in Missouri. After serving as a slave driver, he was hired out to transport slaves to the New Orleans slave market, but managed to escape. Here he describes the punishments he encountered while he was a slave in Missouri.

My mother was hired out in the city, and I was also hired out there to Major Freeland, who kept a public house. He was formerly from Virginia, and was a horse-racer, cock-fighter, gambler, and withal an inveterate drunkard. There were ten or twelve servants in the house, and when he was present, it was cut and slash— knock down and drag out. In his fits of anger, he would take up a chair, and throw it at a servant; and in his more rational moments, when he wished to chastise one, he would tie them up in the smokehouse, and whip them; after which, he would cause a fire to be made of tobacco stems, and smoke them. This he called "Virginia play."

I complained to my master of the treatment which I received from Major Freeland; but it made no difference. He cared nothing about it, so long as he received the money for my labor. After living with Major Freeland five or six months, I ran away, and went into the woods back of the city; and when night came on, I made my way to my master's farm, knowing that if Mr. Haskell, the overseer, should discover me, I should be again carried back to Major Freeland; so I kept in the woods. One day, while in the woods, I heard the barking and howling of dogs, and in a short time they came so near that I knew them to be the bloodhounds of Major

Source: *Narrative of William W. Brown, A Fugitive Slave* (Boston, 1847).

Benjamin O'Fallon. He kept five or six, to hunt runaway slaves with.

As soon as I was convinced that it was them, I knew there was no chance of escape. I took refuge in the top of a tree and the hounds were soon at its base, and there remained until the hunters came up in a half or three quarters of an hour afterwards. There were two men with the dogs, who, as soon as they came up, ordered me to descend. I came down, was tied, and taken to St. Louis jail. Major Freeland soon made his appearance, and took me out, and ordered me to follow him, which I did. After we returned home I was tied up in the smokehouse, and was very severely whipped. After the major had flogged me to his satisfaction, he sent out his son Robert, a young man eighteen or twenty years of age, to see that I was well smoked. He made a fire of tobacco stems, which soon set me to coughing and sneezing. This, Robert told me, was the way his father used to do to his slaves in Virginia. After giving me what they conceived to be a decent smoking, I was untied and again set to work.

29
Moses Roper

"AMONG THE INSTRUMENTS OF TORTURE EMPLOYED"

Moses Roper, who was born into slavery in Caswell County, North Carolina, lived in North and South Carolina and in Georgia before he successfully fled to the North and then to England. In this selection from his autobiography, he describes the punishment he faced after he tried unsuccessfully to run away.

My master gave me a hearty dinner, the best he ever did give me; but it was to keep me from dying before he had given me all the flogging he intended. After dinner he took me up to the log-house, stripped me quite naked, fasted a rail up very high, tied my hands to the rail, fastened my feet together, put a rail between my feet, and stood on the end of it to hold me down; the two sons then gave me fifty lashes, the son-in-law another fifty, and Mr. Gooch himself fifty more.

While doing this his wife came out, and begged him not to kill me, the first act of sympathy I ever noticed in her. When I called for water, they brought a pail-full and threw it over my back ploughed up by the lashes. After this, they took me to the blacksmith's shop, got two large bars of iron, which they bent around my feet, each bar weighing twenty pounds, and put a heavy log-chain on my neck. . . .

Among the instruments of torture employed, I here describe one:—This is a machine used for packing and pressing cotton. By it he hung me up by the hands, a horse, and at times, a man moving round the screw and carrying it up and down, and pressing the block into a box into which the cotton is put. At this time he hung

Source: Moses Roper, *Narrative of the Adventures and Escape of Moses Roper* (London, 1837).

me up for a quarter of an hour. I was carried up ten feet from the ground. . . . After this torture, I stayed with him several months, and did my work very well. It was about the beginning of 1832, when he took off my irons, and being in dread of him, he having threatened me with more punishment, I attempted again to escape from him. At this time I got into North Carolina: but a reward having been offered for me, a Mr. Robinson caught me, and chained me to a chair, upon which he sat up with me all night, and next day proceeded home with me. This was Saturday. Mr. Gooch had gone to church, several miles from his house. When he came back, the first thing he did was to pour some tar upon my head, then rubbed it all over my face, took a torch with pitch on, and set it on fire; he put it out before it did me very great injury, but the pain which I endured was the most excruciating, nearly all my hair having been burnt off. On Monday, he puts irons on me again, weighing nearly fifty pounds. He threatened me again on the Sunday with another flogging; and on the Monday morning, before daybreak, I got away again, with my irons on, and was about three hours going a distance of two miles. I had gone a good distance, when I met with a coloured man, who got some wedges, and took my irons off. However, I was caught again, and put into prison in Charlotte, where Mr. Gooch came, and took me back to Chester. He asked me how I got my irons off. They having been got off by a slave, I would not answer his question, for fear of getting the man punished. Upon this he put the fingers of my hands into a vice, and squeezed all the nails off. He then had my feet put on an anvil, and ordered a man to beat my toes, till he smashed some of my nails off. The marks of this treatment still remain upon me, some of my nails never having grown perfect since.

30
Lewis Clarke

"HER INVENTION WAS WONDERFULLY QUICK"

As a slave child in Kentucky, Lewis Clarke was frequently whipped by his mistress. Here he describes the implements she used to punish him.

[My mistress's] instruments of torture were ordinarily the raw hide, or a bunch of hickory-sprouts seasoned in the fire and tied together. But if these were not at hand, nothing came amiss. She could relish a beating with a chair, the broom, tongs, shovel, shears, knife-handle, the heavy heel of her slipper, or a bunch of keys; her zeal was so active in these barbarous inflictions, that her invention was wonderfully quick, and some way of inflicting the requisite torture was soon found.

One instrument of torture is worthy of particular description. This was an oak club, a foot and a half in length, and an inch and a half square. With this delicate weapon she would beat us upon the hands and upon the feet until they were blistered. This instrument was carefully preserved for a period of four years. Every day, for that time, I was compelled to see that hated tool of cruelty lying in the chair by my side. The least degree of delinquency, either in not doing all the appointed work, or in look or behavior, was visited with a beating from this oak club. That club will always be a prominent object in the picture of horrors of my life of more than twenty years of bitter bondage. . . .

Mrs. Banton, as is common among slave-holding women, seemed to hate and abuse me all the more, because I had some of the blood of her father in my veins. There are no slaves that are so badly abused, as those that are related to some of the women, or the children of their own husband; it seems as though they never could hate these quite bad enough.

Source: *Interesting Memoirs and Documents Relating to American Slavery, and the Glorious Struggle Now Making for Complete Emancipation* (London, 1846).

125

Part 9

RESISTANCE:
"My Lord Says He's Gwineter Rain Down Fire"

Four times during the first thirty-one years of the nineteenth century, American slaves organized insurrections against slavery. In 1800, a twenty-four-year-old Virginia slave named Gabriel Prosser, a blacksmith, led a march of perhaps fifty armed slaves on Richmond. The plot failed when a storm washed out the road to Richmond, giving the Virginia militia time to arrest the rebels. White authorities executed Prosser and twenty-five other conspirators.

In 1811 in Louisiana, between 180 and 500 slaves led by Charles Deslondes, a free mulatto from Haiti, marched on New Orleans, armed with axes and other weapons. Slaveowners retaliated by killing 82 blacks and placing the heads of 16 leaders on pikes.

In 1822, a former slave named Denmark Vesey devised a scheme to take over Charleston, South Carolina, on a summer Sunday when many whites would be vacationing outside the city. Vesey, who had been born either in Africa or the Caribbean in the late 1760s, had won a lottery, purchased his freedom, and opened a carpentry shop. The decision by Charleston authorities to close the city's independent African church led Vesey to organize his conspiracy. Before the revolt could take place, however, a slave betrayed Vesey's plans. The authorities proceeded to arrest 131 blacks and hang 37.

The bloodiest slave revolt in American history took place in 1831 when Nat Turner, a Baptist preacher, led a force of between 60 and 80 slaves on a rampage through Southampton County in southern Virginia, leaving more than 50 whites dead. White authorities retaliated by killing about a hundred blacks. Twenty more slaves, including Turner, were later executed.

Recognizing that open revolt against slavery was futile, most slaves expressed their opposition in more subtle ways, including sabotage, stealing, malingering, murder, arson, and infanticide. These acts of resistance most commonly occurred when a master or overseer overstepped customary bonds. Through these acts, slaves established a right to proper treatment.

31
Frederick Douglass

"COWARDICE DEPARTED, BOLD DEFIANCE TOOK ITS PLACE"

In this selection, Frederick Douglass describes his battles with a "Negro-breaker."

If at any one time of my life more than another, I was made to drink the bitterest dregs of slavery, that time was during the first six months of my stay with Mr. [Edward] Covey. We were worked in all weathers. It was never too hot or too cold; it could never rain, blow, hail, or snow too hard for us to work in the field. Work, work, work was scarcely more the order of the day than of the night. The longest days were too short for him, and the shortest nights too long for him. I was somewhat unmanageable when I first went there, but a few months of this discipline tamed me. Mr. Covey succeeded in breaking me. I was broken in body, soul, and spirit. My natural elasticity was crushed, my intellect languished, the disposition to read departed, the cheerful spark that lingered about my eye died; the dark night of slavery closed in upon me; and behold a man transformed into a brute!

Sunday was my only leisure time. I spent this in a sort of beast-like stupor, between sleep and wake, under some large tree. At times I would rise up, a flash of energetic freedom would dart through my soul, accompanied with a faint gleam of hope that flickered for a moment, and then vanished. I sank down again, mourning over my wretched condition. I was sometimes prompted to take my life and that of Covey, but was prevented by a combination of hope and fear. . . .

You have seen how a man was made a slave; you shall see how a slave was made a man. On one of the hottest days of the

Source: Frederick Douglass, *Narrative of the Life of Frederick Douglass, An American Slave* (Boston, 1845).

month of August, 1833, Bill Smith, William Hughes, a slave named
Eli, and myself were engaged in fanning wheat. . . . The work was
simple, requiring strength rather than intellect; yet, to one entirely
unused to such work, it came very hard. About three o'clock of that
day, I broke down; my strength failed me; I was seized with a violent aching of the head, attended with extreme dizziness; I trembled in every limb. . . .

Mr. Covey was at the house, about one hundred yards from
the treading-yard where we were fanning. On hearing the fan stop,
he left immediately, and came to the spot where we were. He hastily enquired what the matter was. Bill answered that I was sick,
and there was no one to bring wheat to the fan. I had by this time
crawled away under the side of the post and rail-fence by which
the yard was enclosed, hoping to find relief by getting out of the
sun. He then asked where I was. He was told by one of the hands.
He came to the spot, and after looking at me awhile, asked me
what was the matter. I told him as well as I could, for I scarce had
strength to speak. He then gave me a savage kick in the side, and
told me to get up. I tried to do so, but fell back in the attempt. He
gave me another kick, and again told me to rise. I again tried, and
succeeded in gaining my feet: but, stopping to get the tub with
which I was feeding the fan, I again staggered and fell. While down
in this situation, Mr. Covey took up the hickory slat with which
Hughes had been striking off the half-bushel measure, and with it
gave me a heavy blow upon the head, making a large wound, and
the blood ran freely; and with this, again told me to get up. I made
no effort to comply, having now made up my mind to let him do
his worst. In a short time after receiving this blow, my head grew
better. Mr. Covey had now left me to my fate. At this moment I
resolved to go to my master, enter a complaint, and ask his protection. In order to do this, I must that afternoon walk seven miles;
and this, under the circumstances, was truly a severe undertaking.
I was exceedingly feeble; made so as much by the kicks and blows
which I received, as by the severe fit of sickness to which I had been
subjected. I, however, watched my chance, while Covey was looking in an opposite direction, and started for St. Michael's. I succeeded in getting a considerable distance on my way to the woods,
when Covey discovered me, and called after me to come back,
threatening what he would do if I did not come. I disregarded both
his calls and his threats, and made my way to the woods as fast as
my feeble state would allow; and thinking I might be overhauled
by him if I kept the road, I walked through the woods, keeping far
enough from the road to avoid detection, and near enough to pre-

vent losing my way. I had not gone far, before my little strength again failed me. I could go no farther. I fell down, and lay for a considerable time. The blood was yet oozing from the wound on my head. For a time I thought I should bleed to death, and think now that I should have done so, but the blood so matted my hair as to stop the wound. After lying there about three quarters of an hour, I nerved myself up again, and started on my way, through bogs and briers, barefooted and bareheaded, tearing my feet sometimes at nearly every step; and after a journey of about seven miles, occupying some five hours to perform it, I arrived at master's store. I then presented an appearance enough to affect any but a heart of iron. From the crown of my head to my feet, I was covered with blood. My hair was all clotted with dust and blood, my shirt was stiff with briers and thorns, and were also covered with blood. I supposed I looked like a man who had escaped a den of wild beasts, and barely escaped them. In this state I appeared before my master, humbling entreating him to interpose his authority for my protection. I told him all the circumstances as well as I could, and it seemed, as I spoke, at times to affect him. he would then walk the floor, and seek to justify Covey by saying he expected I deserved it. He asked me what I wanted. I told him to let me get a new home; that as sure as I lived with Mr. Covey again, I should live with but to die with him; that Covey would surely kill me—he was in a fair way for it. Master Thomas ridiculed the idea that there was any danger of Mr. Covey's killing me, and said that he knew Mr. Covey; that he was a good man, and that he could not think of taking me from him; that should he do so, he would lose the whole year's wages; that I belonged to Mr. Covey for one year, and that I must go back to him, come what might; and that I must not trouble him with any more stories, or that he would get hold of me. After threatening me thus, he gave me a very large dose of salts, telling me that I might remain in St. Michael's that night, (it being quite late,) but that I must be off back to Mr. Covey's early in the morning; and that if I did not, he would get hold of me, which meant that he would whip me. I remained all night, and according to his orders, I started off to Covey's in the morning (Saturday morning) wearied in body and broken in spirit. I got no supper that night, or breakfast that morning. I reached Covey's about nine o'clock; and just as I was getting over the fence that divided Mrs. Kemp's fields from ours, out ran Covey with his cowskin, to give me another whipping. Before he could reach me, I succeeded in getting to the cornfield; and as the corn was very high, it afforded me the means of hiding. He seemed very angry, and searched for me a long time.

My behaviour was altogether unaccountable. He finally gave up the chase, thinking, I suppose, that I must come home for something to eat; he would give himself no further trouble in looking for me. I spent that day mostly in the woods, having the alternative before me,—to go home and be whipped to death, or stay in the woods and be starved to death. That night, I fell in with Sandy Jenkins, a slave with whom I was somewhat acquainted. Sandy had a free wife, who lived about four miles from Mr. Covey's; and it being Saturday, he was on his way home to see her. I told him my circumstances, and he very kindly invited me to go home with him. I went home with him, and talked this whole matter over, and got his advice as to what course it was best for me to pursue. I found Sandy an old adviser. He told me, with great solemnity, I must go back to Covey; but that before I went, I must go with him into another part of the woods, where there was a certain root, which, if I would take some of it with me, carrying it always on my right side, would render it impossible for Mr. Covey, or any other white man, to whip me. He said he had carried it for years; and since he had done so, he had never received a blow, and never expected to, while he carried it. I at first rejected the idea, that the simple carrying of a root in my pocket would have any such effect as he had said, and was not disposed to take it; but Sandy impressed the necessity with such earnestness, telling me it could do no harm, if it did not good. To please him, I at length took the root, and, according to his direction, carried it upon my right side. This was Sunday morning. I immediately started for home; and upon entering the yard gate, out came Mr. Covey on his way to meeting. He spoke to me very kindly, bade me drive the pigs from a lot near by, and passed toward the church. Now this singular conduct of Mr. Covey really made me begin to think that there was something in the root which Sandy had given me; and had it been any other day than Sunday, I could have attributed the conduct to no other cause than the influence of that root; and as it was, I was half inclined to think the root to be something more than I at first had taken it to be. All went well till Monday morning. On this morning, the virtue of the root was fully tested. Long before daylight, I was called to go and rub, curry, and feed the horses. I obeyed, and was glad to obey. But whilst thus engaged, whilst in the act of throwing down some blades from the loft, Mr. Covey entered the stable with a long rope; and just as I was half way out of the loft, he caught hold of my legs, and was about tying me. As soon as I found what he was up to, I gave a sudden spring, and as I did so, he holding to my legs, I was brought sprawling on the stable floor. Mr. Covey seemed now to think he had me, and could do what he pleased; but at this moment—from whence came the spirit I don't know—I resolved to fight; and suiting my action to the resolution, I seized Covey hard by the throat; and as I did so, I rose. He held on to me, and I to him. My resistance was so entirely unexpected, that Covey seemed taken all aback. He trembled like a leaf. This gave me assurance, and I held him uneasy, causing the blood to run where I touched him with the ends of my fingers. Mr. Covey soon called out to Hughes for help. Hughes came, and, while Covey held me, attempted to tie my right hand. While he was in the act of doing so, I watched my chance, and gave him a heavy kick close under the ribs. This kick fairly sickened Hughes, so that he left me in the hands of Mr. Covey. This kick had the effect of not only weakening Hughes, but Covey also. While he saw Hughes bending over with pain, his courage quailed. He asked me if I meant to persist in my resistance. I told him I did, come what might; that he had used me like a brute for six months, and that I was determined to be used so no longer. With that, he strove to drag me to a stick that was lying just out of the stable door. He meant to knock me down. But just as he was leaning over to get the stick, I seized him with both hands by his collar, and brought him by a sudden snatch to the ground. By this time, Bill came. Covey called upon him for assistance, Bill wanted to know what he could do. Covey said, "Take hold of him, take hold of him!" Bill said his master hired him out to work, and not to help to whip me; so he left Covey and myself to fight our own battle out. We were at it for nearly two hours. Covey at length let me go, puffing and blowing at a great rate, saying that if I had not resisted, he would not have whipped me half so much. The truth was, that he had not whipped me at all. I considered him as getting entirely the worst end of the bargain; for he had drawn no blood from me, but I had from him. The whole six months afterwards, that I spent with Mr. Covey, he never laid the weight of his finger upon me in anger. He would occasionally say, he didn't want to get hold of me again. "No," thought I, "you need not; for you will come off worse than you did before."

This battle with Mr. Covey was the turning-point in my career as a slave. It rekindled the few expiring embers of freedom, and revived within me a sense of my own manhood. It recalled the departed self-confidence, and inspired me again with a determination to be free. The gratification afforded by the triumph was a full compensation for whatever else might follow, even death itself. He only can understand the deep satisfaction which I experienced, who had himself repelled by force the bloody arm of slavery. I felt as I never felt before. It was a glorious resurrection from the tomb of slavery to the heaven of freedom. My long-crushed spirit rose, cowardice departed, bold defiance took its place; and now I resolved that, however long I might remain a slave in form, the day had passed forever when I could be a slave in fact. I did not hesitate to let it be known of me, that the white man who expected to succeed in whipping, must also succeed in killing me.

From this time I was never again what might be called fairly whipped, though I remained a slave four years afterwards. I had several fights, but was never whipped.

It was for a long time a matter of surprise to me why Mr. Covey did not immediately have me taken by the constable to the whipping-post, and there regularly whipped for the crime of raising my hand against a white man in defence of myself. And the only explanation I can now think of does not entirely satisfy me; but such as it is, I will give it. Mr. Covey enjoyed the most unbounded reputation for being a first-rate overseer and Negro-breaker. It was of considerable importance to him. That reputation was at stake; and had he sent me—a boy of sixteen years old—to the whipping-post, his reputation would have been lost; so, to save his reputation, he suffered me to go unpunished.

32
Nat Turner

"THE LAST SHOULD BE FIRST"

In response to questions from a white lawyer named Thomas R. Gray, Nat Turner explains why he led his revolt against slavery.

Sir—You have asked me to give a history of the motives which induced me to undertake the late insurrection, as you call it—To do so I must go back to the days of my infancy.... In my childhood a circumstance occurred which made an indelible impression on my mind, and laid the groundwork of that enthusiasm, which has terminated so fatally to many, both white and black, and for which I am about to atone at the gallows.... Being at play with other children, when three or four years old, I was telling them something, which my mother overhearing, said it had happened before I was born ... others being called on were greatly astonished ... and caused them to say in my hearing, I surely would be a prophet....

For two years [I] prayed continually, whenever my duty would permit—and then again I had ... [a] ... revelation, which fully confirmed me in the impression that I was ordained for some great purpose, in the hands of the Almighty....

About this time [around 1825] I had a vision—and I saw white spirits and black spirits engaged in battle, and the sun was darkened—the thunder rolled in the Heavens, and blood flowed in streams....

And on the 12th of May, 1828, I heard a loud noise in the heavens, and the Spirit instantly appeared to me and said the Serpent was loosened, and Christ had laid down the yoke he had borne for the sins of men, and that I should take it on and fight against the

Source: *The Confessions of Nat Turner, the Leader of the Late Insurrection in Southampton, Va.* (Baltimore, 1831).

Serpent, for the time was fast approaching when the first should be last and the last should be first.

[Question] Do you not find yourself mistaken now?

[Answer] Was not Christ crucified? And by signs in the heavens that it would be made known to me when I should commence the great work—and until the first sign appeared, I should conceal it from the knowledge of men—And on the appearance of the sign (the eclipse of the sun last February), I should arise and prepare myself, and slay my enemies with their own weapons. And immediately on the sign appearing in the heavens, the seal was removed from my lips, and I communicated the great work laid out before me to do, to four in whom I had the greatest confidence (Henry, Hark, Nelson, and Sam)—It was intended by us to have begun the work of death on the 4th of July last—Many were the plans formed and rejected by us, and it affected my mind to such a degree, that I fell sick, and the time passed without our coming to any determination how to commence—Still forming new schemes and rejecting them, when the sign appeared again, which determined me not to wait longer.

Since the commencement of 1830, I had been living with Mr. Joseph Travis, who was to me a kind master, and placed the greatest confidence in me: in fact, I had no cause to complain of his treatment of me. On Saturday evening, the 20th of August, it was agreed between Henry, Hark, and myself, to prepare a dinner the next day for the men we expected, and then to concert a plan, as we had not yet determined on any. Hark, on the following morning, brought a pig, and Henry brandy, and being joined by Sam, Nelson, Will and Jack, they prepared in the woods a dinner, where, about three o'clock, I joined them. . . .

I saluted them on coming up, and asked Will how came he there, he answered, his life was worth no more than others, and his liberty as dear to him. I asked him if he thought to obtain it? He said he would, or lose his life. This was enough to put him in full confidence. Jack, I knew, was only a tool in the hands of Hark, it was quickly agreed we should commence at home (Mr. J. Travis') on that night, and until we had armed and equipped ourselves, and gathered sufficient force, neither age nor sex was to be spared (which was invariably adhered to). We remained at the feast, until about two hours in the night, when we went to the house and found Austin; they all went to the cider press and drank, except myself. On returning to the house Hark went to the door with an axe, for the purpose of breaking it open, as we knew we were strong enough to murder the family, if they were awakened by the noise; but reflecting that it might create an alarm in the neighborhood, we determined to enter the house secretly, and murder them whilst sleeping. Hark got a ladder and set it against the chimney, on which I ascended, and hoisting a window, entered and came down stairs, unbarred the door, and removed the guns from their places. It was then observed that I must spill the first blood. On which, armed with a hatchet, and accompanied by Will, I entered my master's chamber, it being dark, I could not give a death blow, the hatchet glanced from his head, he sprang from the bed and called his wife, it was his last word, Will laid him dead, with a blow of his axe, and Mrs. Travis shared the same fate, as she lay in bed. The murder of this family, five in number, was the work of a moment, not one of them awoke; there was a little infant sleeping in a cradle, that was forgotten, until we had left the house and gone some distance, when Henry and Will returned and killed it; we got here, four guns that would shoot and several old muskets, with a pound or two of powder. We remained some time at the barn, where we paraded; I formed them in a line as soldiers, and ... marched them off to Mr. Salthul Francis', about six hundred yards distant. Sam and Will went to the door and knocked. Mr. Francis asked who was there, Sam replied it was him, and he had a letter for him, on which he got up and came to the door; they immediately seized him, and dragging him out a little from the door, he was dispatched by repeated blows on the head; there was no other white person in the family. We started from there for Mrs. Reese's, maintaining the most perfect silence on our march, where finding the door unlocked, we entered, and murdered Mrs. Reese in her bed, while sleeping; her son awoke, but it was only to sleep the sleep of death, he had only time to say who is that, and he was no more. From Mrs. Reese's we went to Mrs. Turner's, a mile distant, which we reached about sunrise, on Monday morning. Henry, Austin, and Sam, went to the still, where, finding Mr. Peebles, Austin shot him, and the rest of us went to the house; as we approached, the family discovered us, and shut the door. Vain hope! Will, with one stroke of his axe opened it, and we entered and found Mrs. Turner and Mrs. Newsome in the middle of a room, almost frightened to death. Will immediately killed Mrs. Turner, with one blow of his axe. I took Mrs. Newsome by the hand, and with the sword I had when I was apprehended, I struck her several blows over the head, but not being able to kill her, as the sword was dull. Will turning around and discovering it, dispatched her also. A general destruction of property and search for money and ammunition, always succeeded the murders. By this time my company amounted to fifteen, and nine men mounted, who started for Mrs. Whitehead's. . . . As we approached the house we discovered Mr. Richard Whitehead standing in the cotton patch, near the lane fence; we called him over into the lane, and Will, the executioner, was near at hand, with his fatal axe, to send him to an untimely grave. . . . As I came around to the door I saw Will pulling Mrs. Whitehead out of the house, and at the step he nearly severed her head from her body, with his broad axe. Miss Margaret, when I discovered her, had concealed herself in the corner . . . on my approach she fled, but was soon overtaken, and after repeated blows with a sword, I killed her by a blow on the head, with a fence rail. . . .

. . . 'Twas my object to carry terror and devastation wherever we went. . . . I sometimes got in sight in time to see the work of death completed, viewed the mangled bodies as they lay, in silent satisfaction, and immediately started in quest of other victims— Having murdered Mrs. Waller and ten children, we started for Mr. William Williams'—having killed him and two little boys that were there; while engaged in this, Mrs. Williams fled and got some distance from the house, but she was pursued, overtaken, and compelled to get up behind one of the company, who brought her back, and after showing her the mangled body of her lifeless husband, she was told to get down an lay by his side, where she was shot dead. . . .

Our number amounted now to fifty or sixty, all mounted and armed with guns, axes, swords, and clubs. . . . We were met by a party of white men, who had pursued our blood-stained track. . . . The white men, eighteen in number, approached us in about one hundred yards, when one of them fired. . . . I then ordered my men to fire and rush them; the few remaining stood their ground until we approached within fifty yards, when they fired and retreated. . . . As I saw them re-loading their guns, and more coming up than I saw at first, and several of my bravest men being wounded, the others became panick struck and squandered over the field; the white men pursued and fired on us several times. . . .

All deserted me but two, (Jacob and Nat,) we concealed ourselves in the woods until near night, when I sent them in search of Henry, Sam, Nelson, and Hark, and directed them to rally all they could, at the place where we had our dinner the Sunday before, where they would find me, and I accordingly returned there as soon as it was dark and remained until Wednesday evening, when discovering white men riding around the place as though they were looking for someone, and none of my men joining me, I concluded Jacob and Nat had been taken, and compelled to betray me. On this I gave up all hope for the present; and on Thursday night after having supplied myself with provisions from Mr. Travis' I scratched a hole under a pile of fence rails in a field, where I concealed myself for six weeks, never leaving my hiding place but for a few minutes in the dead of night to get water which was very near.... I know not how long I might have led this life, if accident had not betrayed me, a dog in the neighborhood passing by my hiding place one night while I was out, was attracted by some meat I had in my cave, and crawled in and stole it, and was coming out just as I returned. A few nights after, two Negroes having started to go hunting with the same dog, and passed that way, the dog came again to the place, and having just gone out to walk about, discovered me and barked, on which thinking myself discovered, I spoke to them to beg concealment. On making myself known they fled from me. Knowing then they would betray me, I immediately left my hiding place, and was pursued almost incessantly until I was taken a fortnight afterwards by Mr. Benjamin Phipps, in a little hole I had dug out with my sword, for the purpose of concealment, under the top of a fallen tree.

Part 10

FLIGHT:

"Follow the Drinkin' Gourd"

The images are indelibly etched in the American mind: fugitive slaves traveling furtively under cover of darkness, pursued by heavily armed slave catchers and vicious bloodhounds, assisted by benevolent abolitionists who hide them in haystacks and secret rooms and lead them to freedom. Few myths exert a more powerful hold on the American imagination than the underground railroad. But as historian Larry Gara first demonstrated a generation ago, the underground railroad was more a myth than a reality.

Most runaways fled only a short distance. Slaves might hide in nearby swamps to escape punishment or sale. Many slaves ran away to visit spouses or children. Groups of slaves might run away temporarily to protest overwork or cruel punishment. Those fugitives who were trying to escape slavery did not necessarily flee northward. Many headed toward Florida or to the Great Dismal Swamp in Virginia and North Carolina, where they established "maroon" colonies. Others hid in southern cities.

The number of slaves who escaped from slavery was probably about a thousand a year. And, for the most part, these fugitives could not depend on an organized system of underground railroad stations to ferry them to freedom. While some abolitionists like Levi Coffin, William Still, and Harriet Tubman actively assisted fugitives, most runaways had to rely on their own wits. They had to borrow or forge passes, devise disguises, locate hiding places, or stow away on boats or trains. As one Illinois abolitionist later pointed out: "I do not know of any fugitive ever being transported by anyone, they always had to pilot their own canoe, with the little help that they received."

33
Margaret Ward

"SHE WOULD NOT BE WHIPPED, SHE WOULD RATHER DIE"

Margaret Ward and her infant son Samuel Ringgold Ward, slaves from Maryland, follow the North Star to freedom.

At sixteen she went to live with her young mistress, who was married to a planter in that fertile country known as the "Eastern Shore." At eighteen Margaret was a large woman, tall and well formed, her complexion black as jet, her countenance always pleasant, though she seldom laughed. She talked but little, even to those of her own race. At twenty years of age she became the wife of a worthy young man to whom she had given her best affections. Not long after, her young master became very angry with her for what he called stubbornness and resistance to his will, and threatened to chastise her by whipping—a degradation that she had always felt that she could not submit to, and yet to obey her master in the thing he demanded would be still worse. She therefore told him that she would not be whipped, she would rather die, and gave him warning that any attempt to execute his threat would surely result in the death of one of them. He knew her too well to risk the experiment, and decided to punish her in another way. He sold her husband, and she saw him bound in chains and driven off with a large drove of men and women for the New Orleans market. He then put her in the hands of a brutal overseer, with directions to work her to the extent of her ability on a tobacco plantation, which command was enforced up to the day of the birth of her child. At the end of one week she was driven again to the field and compelled to perform a full task, having at no time any abatement of her work on account of her situation, with exception of one week.

Source: Eber Pettit, *Sketches in the History of the Underground Railroad* (Fredonia, N.Y., 1879).

It was the custom on the plantation to establish nurseries, presided over by old, broken down slaves, where mothers might leave their infants, but this privilege was denied to Margaret. She was obliged to leave her child under the shade of a bush in the field, returning to it but twice during the long day. On returning to the child one evening she found it apparently senseless, exhausted with crying, and a large serpent lying across it. Although she felt that it would be better for both herself and child if it were dead, yet a mother's heart impelled her to make an effort to save it, and by caressing him and careful handling she resuscitated it.

As soon as she heard its feeble, wailing cry, she made a vow to deliver her boy from the cruel power of slavery or die in the attempt, and falling prostrate, she prayed for strength to perform her vow, and for grace and patience to sustain her in her suffering, toil, and hunger; then pressing her child to her bosom, she fled with all the speed of which she was capable toward the North Star. Having gone a mile or two, she heard something pursuing her; on looking round she saw Watch, the old house dog. Watch was a large mastiff, somewhat old, and with him Margaret had ever been a favorite, and since she had been driven to the field, Watch often visited her at her cabin in the evening. She feared it would not be safe to allow Watch to go with her, but she could not induce him to go back, so she resumed her flight, accompanied by her faithful escort. At break of day she hid herself on the border of a plantation and soon fell asleep.

Toward evening she was aroused by the noise made by the slaves returning to their quarters, and seeing an old woman lingering behind all the others, she called her, told her troubles, and asked for food. The old woman returned about midnight with a pretty good supply of food, which Margaret divided with Watch, and then started on, taking the North Star for her guide. The second day after she left, the Overseer employed a hunter with his dogs to find her. He started with an old slut and three whelps, thinking, no doubt, that as the game was only a woman and her infant child, it would be a good time to train his pups.

Margaret had been missed at roll call the morning after her flight, but the Overseer supposed she was hiding near the place for a day or two, and that hunger would soon drive her up; therefore, when the hunter started, he led the old dog, expecting to find her in an hour or two, but not overtaking her the first day, on the next morning, he let his hounds loose, intending to follow on horseback, guided by their voices. About noon, the old dog struck the track at the place where Margaret had made her little camp the day before, and she bounded off with fresh vigor, leaving the man and the younger dogs beyond sight and hearing. The young dogs soon lost the track where Margaret forded the streams, and the old dog was miles away, leaving the hunter without a guide to direct him.

Margaret had been lying in the woods on the bank of a river, intending to start again as soon as it was dark, when she was startled by the whining and nervous motions of old Watch, and listening, she heard the hoarse ringing bay of a blood-hound. Although she had expected that she would be hunted with dogs, and recalled over and over again the shocking accounts related by Overseers to the slaves, of fugitives overtaken and torn in pieces by the savage Spanish blood-hounds, she had not, until now, realized the horrors of her situation. She expected to have to witness the destruction of her child by the savage brute, and then be torn in pieces herself. Meanwhile, old Watch lay with his nose between his feet, facing the coming foe. The hound, rendered more fierce by the freshness of the track, came rushing headlong with nose to the ground, scenting her prey, and seemed not to see old Watch, until, leaping to pass over him, she found her wind-pipe suddenly collapsed in the massive jaws of the old mastiff. The struggle was not very noisy, for Watch would not even growl, and the hound could not, for it was terribly energetic. The hound made rapid and persuasive gestures with her paws and tail, but it was of no use, the jaws of old Watch relaxed not until all signs of life in his enemy had ceased. Margaret came back from the river, and would have embraced her faithful friend, but fearing that a stronger pack was following, she hastily threw the dead hound into the river and pursued her journey.

Within a few hours after her providential escape by the aid of her faithful friend, old Watch, from the fangs of the slave hunter's hound, she fell into the hands of friends, who kept her secreted until she could be sent into a free State; while there, she learned about the pursuit by the hunter, and that he never knew what became of his best hound. After the chase was abandoned, she, through a regular line, similar to our Underground Railroad, was sent to Philadelphia and then to New York, where she became a celebrated nurse, and always befriended the poor of all colors and all nationalities.

34
Frederick Douglass

"A NEW WORLD BURST UPON MY AGITATED VISION"

Frederick Douglass uses a black sailor's papers to escape from slavery.

I have never approved of the very public manner, in which some of our Western friends have conducted what they call the "Under-ground Railroad," but which, I think, by their open declarations, has been made, most emphatically, the "Upper-ground Railroad." Its stations are far better known to the slaveholders than to the slaves. I honor those good men and women for their noble daring, in willingly subjecting themselves to persecution, by openly avowing their participation in the escape of slaves; nevertheless, the good resulting from such avowals, is of a very questionable character. It may kindle an enthusiasm, very pleasant to inhale; but that is of no practical benefit to themselves, nor to the slaves escaping. Nothing is more evident, than that such disclosures are a positive evil to the slaves remaining, and seeking to escape. In publishing such accounts, the anti-slavery man addresses the slaveholder, not the slave; he stimulates the former to greater watchfulness, and adds to the facilities for capturing the slave. . . .

My condition in the year [1838] of my escape, was, comparatively, a free and easy one, so far, at least, as the wants of the physical man were concerned; but the reader will bear in mind, that my troubles from the beginning, have been less physical than mental. . . . The practice, from week to week, of openly robbing me of all my earnings, kept the nature and character of slavery constantly before me. I could be robbed by indirection, but this was

Source: Frederick Douglass, *My Bondage and My Freedom* (New York, 1855); Frederick Holland, *Frederick Douglass* (New York, 1895).

too open and barefaced to be endured. I could see no reason why I should, at the end of each week, pour the reward of my honest toil into the purse of any man. . . .

Held to a strict account, and kept under a close watch—the old suspicion of my running away not having been entirely removed—escape from slavery, even in Baltimore, was very difficult. The railroad from Baltimore to Philadelphia was under regulations so stringent, that even free colored travelers were almost excluded. They must have free papers; they must be measured and carefully examined, before they were allowed to enter the cars; they only went in the day time, even when so examined. The steamboats were under regulations equally stringent. All the great turnpikes, leading northward, were beset with kidnappers, a class of men who watched the newspapers for advertisements for runaway slaves, making their living by the accursed reward of slave hunting.

My discontent grew upon me, and I was on the lookout for means of escape. With money, I could easily have managed the matter, and, therefore, I hit upon the plan of soliciting the privilege of hiring my time. It is quite common, in Baltimore, to allow slaves this privilege, and it is the practice, also in New Orleans. A slave who is considered trustworthy, can, by paying his master a definite sum regularly, at the end of each week dispose of his time as he likes. . . .

The laws of Maryland required every free Negro to carry papers describing him accurately and to pay liberally for this protection. Slaves often escaped by borrowing papers from a friend, to whom the precious documents would be returned by mail. Whenever a coloured man came with free papers to the railroad station to buy a ticket, he was always examined carefully enough to insure the detection of a runaway, unless the resemblence was very close. Our hero was not acquainted with any free Negro who looked much like him; but he found out that passengers who paid on the cars were not scrutinized so minutely as those who bought tickets, and also that sailors were treated with peculiar indulgence by the conductors. . . .

Among his friends was a sailor who was of much darker hue than he was himself, but who owned a protection, setting forth his occupation, and bearing the sacred figure of the American eagle. This was borrowed; sailor's clothes were purchased, and on Monday morning, the fugitive jumped on the train just as it started. His baggage had been put aboard by a friendly hackman. He was greatly troubled, for, as he wrote to his master, ten years later, I was making a leap in the dark. The probabilities, so far as I could by reason determine them, were stoutly against the undertaking. The preliminaries and precautions I had adopted previously, all worked badly. I was like one going to war without weapons—ten chances of defeat to one of victory. One in whom I had confided, and one who had promised me assistance, appalled by the fear at the trial hour, deserted me. However, gloomy as was the prospect, thanks be to the Most High, who is ever the God of the oppressed, at the moment which was to determine my whole earthly career, His grace was sufficient; my mind was made up.

His anxiety increased in consequence of the harshness with which the conductor questioned other passengers in the Negro car. The sailor, however, was addressed kindly and told, after a mere glance at the protection, that it was all right. Thus far he was safe; but there were several people on the train who would have known him at once in any other clothes. A German blacksmith looked at him intently, and apparently recognized him, but said nothing. On the ferry boat, by which they crossed the Susquehanna, he found an old acquaintance employed, and was asked some dangerous questions. On they went, however, until they stopped to let the train from Philadelphia pass. At the window sat a man under whom the runaway had been at work but a few days before. He might easily have recognized him, and would certainly have him arrested; but fortunately he was looking another way. The passengers went on from Wilmington by steamer to Philadelphia, where one of them took the train for New York and arrived early on Tuesday. In less than twenty-four hours the slave had made himself a free man. It was but a few months since he had become twenty-one.

The flight was a bold and perilous one; but here I am, in the great city of New York, safe and sound, without loss of blood or bone. In less than a week after leaving Baltimore, I was walking amid the hurrying throng, and gazing upon the dazzling wonders of Broadway. The dreams of my childhood and the purposes of my manhood were now fulfilled. A free state around me, and a free earth under my feet! What a moment was this to me! A whole year was pressed into a single day. A new World burst upon my agitated vision.

35
Harriet Tubman

"THE MOST REMARKABLE WOMAN
OF THIS AGE"

Harriet Tubman, the famous fugitive slave from Maryland, risks her life sneaking into slave territory to free slaves. Slaveholders posted a $40,000 reward for the capture of the "Black Moses."

One of the teachers lately commissioned by the New-England Freedmen's Aid Society is probably the most remarkable woman of this age. That is to say, she has performed more wonderful deeds by the native power of her own spirit against adverse circumstances than any other. She is well known to many by the various names which her eventful life has given her; Harriet Garrison, Gen. Tubman, &c.; but among the slaves she is universally known by her well earned title of Moses,—Moses the deliverer. She is a rare instance, in the midst of high civilization and intellectual culture, of a being of great native powers, working powerfully, and to beneficent ends, entirely untaught by schools or books.

Her maiden name was Araminta Ross. She is the granddaughter of a native African, and has not a drop of white blood in her veins. She was born in 1820 or 1821, on the Eastern Shore of Maryland. . . .

She seldom lived with her owner, but was usually "hired out" to different persons. She once "hired her time," and employed it in the rudest farming labors, ploughing, carting, driving the oxen, &c., to so good advantage that she was able in one year to buy a pair of steers worth forty dollars.

When quite young she lived with a very pious mistress; but the slaveholder's religion did not prevent her from whipping the young girl for every slight or fancied fault. Araminta found that

Source: *Commonwealth* (July 17, 1863); *Freeman's Record* (March 1865).

this was usually a morning exercise; so she prepared for it by putting on all the thick clothes she could procure to protect her skin. She made sufficient outcry, however, to convince her mistress that her blows had full effect; and in the afternoon she would take off her wrappings, and dress as well as she could. When invited into family prayers, she preferred to stay on the landing, and pray for herself; "and I prayed to God," she says "to make me strong and able to fight and that's what I've allers prayed for ever since. . . . "

In her youth she received a severe blow on her head from a heavy weight thrown by her master at another slave, but which accidentally hit her. The blow produced a disease of the brain which was severe for a long time, and still makes her very lethargic. . . . She was married about 1844 to a free colored man named John Tubman, but never had any children. Owing to changes in her owner's family, it was determined to sell her and some other slaves; but her health was so much injured, that a purchaser was not easily found. At length she became convinced that she would soon be carried away, and she decided to escape. Her brothers did not agree with her plans, and she walked off alone, following the guidance of the brooks, which she had observed to run North. . . .

She remained two years in Philadelphia working hard and carefully hoarding her money. Then she hired a room, furnished it as well as she could, bought a nice suit of men's clothes, and went back to Maryland for her husband. But the faithless man had taken to himself another wife. Harriet did not dare venture into her presence, but sent word to her husband where she was. He declined joining her. At first her grief and anger were excessive . . . but finally she thought. . . . "if he could do without her, she could without him," and so "he dropped out of her heart," and she determined to give her life to brave deeds. Thus all personal aims died out of her heart; and with her simple brave motto, "I can't die but once," she began the work which has made her Moses,—the deliverer of her people. Seven or eight times she has returned to the neighborhood of her former home, always at the risk of death in the most terrible forms, and each time has brought away a company of fugitive slaves, and led them safely to the free States, or to Canada. Every time she went, the dangers increased. In 1857, she brought away her old parents, and, as they were too feeble to walk, she was obliged to hire a wagon, which added greatly to the perils of the journey. In 1860 she went for the last time, and among her troop was an infant whom they were obliged to keep stupefied with laudanum to prevent its outcries. . . .

She always came in the winter when the nights are long and

dark, and people who have homes stay in them. She was never seen on the plantation herself; but appointed a rendezvous for her company eight or ten miles distant, so that if they were discovered at the first start she was not compromised. She started on Saturday night; the slaves at that time being allowed to go away from home to visit their friends—so that they would not be missed until Monday morning. Even then they were supposed to have loitered on the way, and it would often be late on Monday afternoon before the flight would be certainly known. If by any further delay the advertisement was not sent out before Tuesday morning, she felt secure of keeping ahead of it; but if it were, it required all her ingenuity to escape. She resorted to various devices, she had confidential friends all along the road. She would hire a man to follow the one who put up the notices, and take them down as soon as his back was turned. She crossed creeks on railroad bridges by night, she hid her company in the woods while she herself not being advertised went into the towns in search of information. . . .

The expedition was governed by the strictest rules. If any man gave out, he must be shot. "Would you really do that?" she was asked. "Yes," she replied, "if he was weak enough to give out, he'd be weak enough to betray us all, and all who had helped us; and do you think I'd let so many die just for one coward man." "Did you ever have to shoot any one?" she was asked. "One time," she said, "a man gave out on the second night; his feet were sore and swollen, he couldn't go any further; he'd rather go back and die, if he must." They tried all arguments in vain, bathed his feet, tried to strengthen him, but it was of no use, he would go back. Then she said, "I told the boys to get their guns ready, and shoot him. They'd have done it in a minute; but when he heard that, he jumped right up and went on as well as any body. . . ."

When going on these journeys she often lay alone in the forests all night. Her whole soul was filled with awe of the mysterious Unseen Presence, which thrilled her with such depths of emotion, that all other care and fear vanished. Then she seemed to speak with her Maker "as a man talketh with his friend;" her child-like petitions had direct answers, and beautiful visions lifted her up above all doubt and anxiety into serene trust and faith. No man can be a hero without this faith in some form; the sense that he walks not in his own strength, but leaning on an almighty arm. Call it fate, destiny, what you will, Moses of old, Moses of to-day, believed it to be Almighty God.

36
Henry "Box" Brown

"HE . . . HIT UPON A
NEW INVENTION ALTOGETHER"

*Henry "Box" Brown escapes slavery by having himself
nailed into a small box and shipped from Richmond to
Philadelphia.*

He was decidedly an unhappy piece of property in the city of
Richmond, Va. In the condition of a slave he felt that it would be
impossible for him to remain. Full well did he know, however, that
it was no holiday task to escape the vigilance of Virginia slave-
hunters, or the wrath of an enraged master for committing the
unpardonable sin of attempting to escape to a land of liberty. So
Brown counted well the cost before venturing upon his hazardous
undertaking. Ordinary modes of travel he concluded might prove
disastrous to his hopes; he, therefore, hit upon a new invention
altogether, which was to have himself boxed up and forwarded to
Philadelphia direct by express. The size of the box and how it was
to be made to fit him most comfortably, was of his own ordering.
Two feet eight inches deep, two feet wide, and three feet long were
the exact dimensions of the box, lined with baize. His resources in
regard to food and water consisted of the following: One bladder of
water and a few small biscuits. His mechanical implement to meet
the death-struggle for fresh air, all told, was one large gimlet. Satisfied that it would be far better to peril his life for freedom in this
way than to remain under the galling yoke of Slavery, he entered
his box, which was safely nailed up and hooped with five hickory
hoops, and then was addressed by his next friend, James A. Smith,
a shoe dealer, to Wm. H. Johnson, Arch Street, Philadelphia,
marked, "This side up with care." In this condition he was sent to
Adams' Express office in a dray, and thence by overland express to

Source: William Still, *Underground Railroad Records* (Philadelphia, 1872).

Philadelphia. It was twenty-six hours from the time he left Richmond until his arrival in the city of Brotherly Love. The notice, "This side up, etc.," did not avail with the different expressmen, who hesitated not to handle the box in the usual rough manner common to this class of men. For a while they actually had the box upside down, and had him on his head for miles. A few days before he was expected, certain intimation was conveyed to a member of the Vigilance Committee that a box might be expected by the three o'clock morning train from the South, which might contain a man.

All was quiet. The door had been safely locked. The proceedings commenced. Mr. [J. M.] McKim rapped quietly on the lid of the box and called out, "All right!" Instantly came the answer from within, "All right, sir!"

The witnesses will never forget that moment, Saw and hatchet quickly had the five hickory hoops cut and the lid off, and the marvelous resurrection of Brown ensued. Rising up in the box, he reached out his hand, saying, "How do you do, gentlemen?" the little assemblage hardly knew what to think or do at the moment. He was about as wet as if he had come up out of the Delaware. Very soon he remarked that, before leaving Richmond he had selected for his arrival hymn (if he lived) the Psalm beginning with these words: "I awaited patiently for the Lord, and He heard my prayer." And most touchingly did he sing the psalm, much to his own relief, as well as to the delight of his small audience.

37
Margaret Garner

"SHE WOULD KILL HERSELF ... BEFORE SHE WOULD RETURN TO BONDAGE"

Margaret Garner, a fugitive slave from Kentucky, killed one of her children rather than permit her to be returned to slavery. She drowned in a shipwreck as she was being brought back to slavery.

Perhaps no case that came under my notice, while engaged in aiding fugitive slaves, attracted more attention and aroused deeper interest and sympathy than the case of Margaret Garner, the slave mother who killed her child rather than see it taken back to slavery. This happened in the latter part of January, 1856. The Ohio River was frozen over at the time, and the opportunity thus offered for escaping to a free State was embraced by a number of slaves living in Kentucky, several miles back from the river. A party of seventeen, belonging to different masters in the same neighborhood, made arrangements to escape together. There was snow on the ground and the roads were smooth, so the plan of going to the river on a sled naturally suggested itself. The time fixed for their flight was Sabbath night, and having managed to get a large sled and two good horses, belonging to one of their masters, the party of seventeen crowded into the sled and started on their hazardous journey in the latter part of the night. They drove the horses at full speed, and at daylight reached the River below Covington, opposite Wester Row. They left the sled and horses here, and as quickly as possible crossed the river on foot. It was now broad daylight, and people were beginning to pass about the streets and the fugitives divided their company that they might not attract so much notice.

An old slave named Simon and his wife Mary, together with

Source: Levi Coffin, *Reminiscences* (Cincinnati, 1876).

their son Robert and his wife Margaret Garner and four children, made their way to the house of a colored man named Kite, who had formerly lived in their neighborhood and had been purchased from slavery by his father, Joe Kite. They had to make several inquiries in order to find Kite's house, which was below Mill Creek, in the lower part of the city. This afterward led to their discovery; they had been seen by a number of persons on their way to Kite's, and were easily traced by pursuers. The other nine fugitives were more fortunate. They made their way up town and found friends who conducted them to safe hiding-places, where they remained until night. They were put on the Underground Railroad, and went safely through to Canada....

In a few minutes ... [Kite's] ... house was surrounded by pursuers—the masters of the fugitives, with officers and a posse of men. The door and windows were barred, and those inside refused to give admittance. The fugitives were determined to fight, and to die, rather than to be taken back to slavery. Margaret, the mother of the four children, declared that she would kill herself and her children before she would return to bondage. The slave men were armed and fought bravely. The window was first battered down with a stick of wood, and one of the deputy marshals attempted to enter, but a pistol shot from within made a flesh wound on his arm and caused him to abandon the attempt. The pursuers then battered down the door with some timber and rushed in. The husband of Margaret fired several shots, and wounded one of the officers, but was soon overpowered and dragged out of the house. At this moment, Margaret Garner, seeing that their hopes of freedom were in vain, seized a butcher knife that lay on the table, and with one stroke cut the throat of her little daughter, whom she probably loved the best. She then attempted to take the life of the other children and to kill herself, but she was overpowered and hampered before she could complete her desperate work. The whole party was then arrested and lodged in jail.

The trial lasted two weeks, drawing crowds to the courtroom every day.... The counsel for the defense brought witnesses to prove that the fugitives had been permitted to visit the city at various times previously. It was claimed that Margaret Garner had been brought here by her owners a number of years before, to act as nurse girl, and according to the law which liberated slaves who were brought into free States by the consent of their masters, she had been free from that time, and her children, all of whom had been born since then—following the condition of the mother—were likewise free.

The Commissioner decided that a voluntary return to slavery, after a visit to a free State, re-attached the conditions of slavery, and that the fugitives were legally slaves at the time of their escape....

But in spite of touching appeals, of eloquent pleadings, the Commissioner remanded the fugitives back to slavery. He said that it was not a question of feeling to be decided by the chance current of his sympathies; the law of Kentucky and the United States made it a question of property.

Part 11

EMANCIPATION:
"The Walls Come Tumblin' Down"

The slave population did not respond to Civil War with a single voice. While Southern planters stressed their bondsmen's loyalty and fidelity, in Adams County, Mississippi, slave insurrectionaries plotted to burn down the city of Natchez. Other slaves served as informants to the Union army, assisted Union soldiers who escaped from Confederate prisons, or defected to Union lines or hid out in nearby woods or swamps. Wartime resistance to slavery also took the form of work stoppages, arson, sabotage, and isolated cases of murder. Enlistment in the Union army represented the most dramatic form of resistance. In August 1862, the first slave regiment was formed, the 1st South Carolina Volunteers, and by the war's end, 186,000 blacks—three-quarters of them former slaves—served in the Union army.

News of emancipation evoked a variety of responses, ranging from exuberance and exhilaration to incredulity and caution to apprehension and fear. In Choctaw County, Mississippi, former slaves whipped a planter named Nat Best to retaliate for his cruelties. In Richmond, Virginia, some 1,500 ex-slaves gathered in the Free African Church to sing hymns. A parade in Charleston attracted 10,000 spectators and featured a black-draped coffin bearing the words "Slavery is Dead." But many freedmen felt a deep uncertainty about their status and rights.

Ex-slaves expressed their newly-won freedom in diverse ways. At first, many left farms or plantations for towns or cities "where freedom was free-er." Thousands sought to reunite families broken by sale and legalize marriage ties; others adopted new surnames and learned to read and write. Many black women withdrew from field labor to care for their families. Across the South, ex-slaves left white-

dominated churches and formed independent black congregations; founded schools; set up mutual aid societies; and held freedmen's conventions to air grievances, discuss pressing issues, and press for equal civil and political rights.

Reconstruction was a time of testing, when freedmen probed the boundaries and possibilities of freedom. Every aspect of Southern life was subject to redefinition, from appropriate forms of racial etiquette to the systems of labor that would replace slavery.

38
Thomas Long

"WE WHIPPED DOWN ALL DAT"

Thomas Long, a former slave and a private in the 1st South Carolina Volunteers, assesses the meaning of black military service during the Civil War.

We can remember, when we fust enlisted, it was hardly safe for we to pass by de camps to Beaufort and back, lest we went in a mob and carried side arms. But we whipped down all dat—not by going into de white camps for whip um; we didn't tote our bayonets for whip um; but we lived it down by our naturally manhood; and now de white sojers take us by de hand and say Broder Sojer. Dats what dis regiment did for de Epiopian race.

If we hadn't become sojers, all might have gone back as it was before; our freedom might have slipped through de two houses of Congress and President Linkum's four years might have passed by and notin' been done for us. But now tings can neber go back, because we have showed our energy and our courage and our naturally manhood.

Source: Thomas Wentworth Higginson, *Army Life in a Black Regiment* (Boston, 1870).

39
Jackson Cherry

"WE OUGHT TO BE CONSIDERED AS MEN"

Corporal Jackson Cherry, Company I, 35th Regiment, United States Colored Troops, appeals for equal opportunity for freedmen.

We have been faithful in the field up to the present time, and think that we ought to be considered as men, and allowed a fair chance in the race of life. It has been said that a black man can not make his own living, but give us opportunities and we will show the whites that we will not come to them for any thing, if they do not come to us. We think the colored people have been the making of them, and can make something of ourselves in time. The colored people know how to work, and the whites have been dependent upon them. They can work again, and will work. A white man may talk very well, but put him to work, and what will he say? He will say that hard work is not easy. He will say that it is hard for a man who has owned so many able-bodied Negroes to have the Yankees come and take them all away.

Source: *South Carolina Leader*, December 16, 1865

40
Jourdon Anderson

"I THOUGHT THE YANKEES WOULD HAVE HUNG YOU LONG BEFORE THIS"

Jourdon Anderson, an ex-Tennessee slave, declines his former master's invitation to return as a laborer on his plantation.

Dayton, Ohio, August 7, 1865

To My Old Master, Colonel P.H. Anderson,
Big Spring, Tennessee

Sir: I got your letter and was glad to find you had not forgotten Jourdon, and that you wanted me to come back and live with you again, promising to do better for me than anybody else can. I have often felt uneasy about you. I thought the Yankees would have hung you long before this for harboring Rebs they found at your house. I suppose they never heard about your going to Col. Martin's to kill the Union soldier that was left by his company in their stable. Although you shot at me twice before I left you, I did not want to hear of your being hurt, and am glad you are still living. It would do me good to go back to the dear old home again and see Miss Mary and Miss Martha and Allen, Esther, Green, and Lee. Give my love to them all, and tell them I hope we will meet in the better world, if not in this. I would have gone back to see you all when I was working in the Nashville hospital, but one of the neighbors told me Henry intended to shoot me if he ever got a chance.

I want to know particularly what the good chance is you pro-

Source: *Cincinnati Commercial,* reprinted in *New York Tribune,* August 22, 1865.

pose to give me. I am doing tolerably well here; I get $25 a month, with victuals and clothing; have a comfortable home for Mandy (the folks here call her Mrs. Anderson), and the children, Milly, Jane and Grundy, go to school and are learning well; the teacher says Grundy has a head for a preacher. They go to Sunday-School, and Mandy and me attend church regularly. We are kindly treated; sometimes we overhear others saying, "The colored people were slaves" down in Tennessee. The children feel hurt when they hear such remarks, but I tell them it was no disgrace in Tennessee to belong to Col. Anderson. Many darkies would have been proud, as I used to be, to call you master. Now, if you will write and say what wages you will give me, I will be better able to decide whether it would be to my advantage to move back again.

As to my freedom, which you say I can have, there is nothing to be gained on that score, as I got my free-papers in 1864 from the Provost-Marshal-General of the Department of Nashville. Mandy says she would be afraid to go back without some proof that you are sincerely disposed to treat us justly and kindly—and we have concluded to test your sincerity by asking you to send us our wages for the time we served you. This will make us forget and forgive old scores, and rely on your justice and friendship in the future. I served you faithfully for thirty-two years and Mandy twenty years. At $25 a month for me, and $2 a week for Mandy, our earnings would amount to $11,680. Add to this the interest for the time our wages has been kept back and deduct what you paid for our clothing and three doctor's visits to me, and pulling a tooth for Mandy, and the balance will show what we are in justice entitled to. Please send the money by Adams Express, in care of V. Winters, esq, Dayton, Ohio. If you fail to pay us for faithful labors in the past we can have little faith in your promises in the future. We trust the good Maker has opened your eyes to the wrongs which you and your fathers have done to me and my fathers, in making us toil for you for generations without recompense. Here I draw my wages every Saturday night, but in Tennessee there was never any pay day for the Negroes any more than for the horses and cows. Surely there will be a day of reckoning for those who defraud the laborer of his hire.

In answering this letter please state if there would be any safety for my Milly and Jane, who are now grown up and both good-looking girls. You know how it was with Matilda and Catherine. I would rather stay here and starve and die if it comes to that than have my girls brought to shame by the violence and wickedness of their young masters. You will also please state if there has been any schools opened for the colored children in your neighborhood, the great desire of my life now is to give my children an education, and have them form virtuous habits.

P.S.—Say howdy to George Carter, and thank him for taking the pistol from you when you were shooting at me.

From your old servant,

Jourdon Anderson

41
Rufus Saxton

"THE WORD 'COLOR' SHOULD BE LEFT OUT OF ALL LAWS"

Major General Rufus Saxton commanded the area that included Georgia's Sea Islands and later became the Freedmen's Bureau's assistant commissioner for Florida, Georgia, and South Carolina. This selection, from his testimony before Congress's Joint Committee on Reconstruction in 1866, offers his assessment of the freedmen's aspirations and the former Confederates' attitudes toward them.

[Question] What is [the freedmen's] disposition in regard to purchasing land, and what is the disposition of the landowners in reference to selling land to Negroes?

[Answer] The object which the freedman has most at heart is the purchase of land. They all desire to get small homesteads and to locate themselves upon them, and there is scarcely any sacrifice too great for them to make to accomplish this object. I believe it is the policy of the majority of the farm owners to prevent Negroes from becoming landholders. They desire to keep the Negroes landless, and as nearly in a condition of slavery as it is possible for them to do. I think that the former slaveholders know really less about the freedmen than any other class of people. The system of slavery has been one of concealment on the part of the Negro of all his feelings and impulses; and that feeling of concealment is so ingrained within the very constitution of the Negro that he deceives his former master on almost every point. The freedman has no faith in his former master, nor has his former owner any faith in the capacity of the freedman. A mutual distrust exists

---

Source: *Report of the Joint Committee on Reconstruction* (Washington, 1866).

between them. But the freedman is ready and willing to contract to work for any northern man. One man from the North, a man of capital, who employed large numbers of freedmen, and paid them regularly, told me, as others have, that he desired no better laborers; that he considered them fully as easy to manage as Irish laborers. That was my own experience in employing several thousands of them in cultivating the soil. I have also had considerable experience in employing white labor, having, as quartermaster, frequently had large numbers of laborers under my control.

[Question] If the Negro is put in possession of all his rights as a man, do you apprehend any danger of insurrection among them?

[Answer] I do not; and I think that is the only thing which will prevent difficulty. I think if the Negro is put in possession of all his rights as a citizen and as a man, he will be peaceful, orderly, and self-sustaining as any other man or class of men, and that he will rapidly advance. . . .

[Question] It has been suggested that, if the Negro is allowed to vote, he will be likely to vote on the side of his former master, and be inveigled in the support of a policy hostile to the government of the United States; do you share in that apprehension?

[Answer] I have positive information from Negroes, from the most intelligent freedmen in those States, those who are leaders among them, that they are thoroughly loyal, and know their friends, and they will never be found voting on the side of oppression. . . . I think it vital to the safety and prosperity of the two races in the South that the Negro should immediately be put in possession of all his rights as a man; and that the word "color" should be left out of all laws, constitutions, and regulations for the people; I think it vital to the safety of the Union that this should be done.

42
Samuel Thomas

"TO KILL A NEGRO
THEY DO NOT DEEM MURDER"

Col. Samuel Thomas, a Freedmen's Bureau official, describes the attitude of ex-Confederates toward the former slaves.

Wherever I go—the street, the shop, the house, or the steamboat—I hear the people talk in such a way as to indicate that they are yet unable to conceive of the Negro as possessing any rights at all. Men who are honorable in their dealings with their white neighbors will cheat a Negro without feeling a single twinge of their honor. To kill a Negro they do not deem murder; to debauch a Negro woman they do not think fornication; to take the property away from a Negro they do not consider robbery. The people boast that when they get freedmen affairs in their own hands, to use their own classic expression, "the niggers will catch hell."

The reason of all this is simple and manifest. The whites esteem the blacks their property by natural right, and however much they may admit that the individual relations of masters and slaves have been destroyed by the war and the President's emancipation proclamation, they still have an ingrained feeling that the blacks at large belong to the whites at large, and whenever opportunity serves they treat the colored people just as their profit, caprice or passion may dictate.

Source: Col. Samuel Thomas, Assistant Commissioner, Bureau of Refugees, Freedmen and Abandoned Lands in 39 Cong., 1 Sess., Senate Exec. Doc. 2 (1865).

43
Francis L. Cardozo

"LET THE LANDS OF THE SOUTH BE ... DIVIDED"

Francis L. Cardozo, a black graduate of the University of Glasgow and a minister in New Haven, Connecticut, returned to his native South Carolina immediately after the Civil War to serve as a principal of a Negro school. In this selection, he calls upon the South Carolina Constitutional Convention to grant land to the freedmen.

One of the greatest of slavery bulwarks was the infernal plantation system, one man owning his thousand, another his twenty, another fifty thousands acres of land. This is the only way by which we will break up that system, and I maintain that our freedom will be of no effect if we allow it to continue. What is the main cause of the prosperity of the North. It is because every man has his own farm and is free and independent. Let the lands of the South be similarly divided. I would not say for one moment they should be confiscated, but if sold to maintain the war, now that slavery is destroyed, let the plantation system go with it. We will never have true freedom until we abolish the system of agriculture which existed in the Southern States. It is useless to have any schools while we maintain the stronghold of slavery as the agricultural system of the country.

Source: Proceedings of Constitution Convention of South Carolina (1868).

167

44

Elias Hill

"THEY HIT ME WITH THEIR FISTS"

Elias Hill, a black minister in York County, South Carolina, testified before a congressional committee in 1871 about the Ku Klux Klan's aims and methods of operation.

Elias Hill is a remarkable character. He is crippled in both legs and arms, which are shriveled by rheumatism; he cannot walk, cannot help himself, has to be fed and cared for personally by others; was in early life a slave, whose freedom was purchased, his father buying his mother and getting Elias along with her, as a burden of which his master was glad to be rid. Stricken at seven years old with disease, he never was afterward able to walk, and he presents the appearance of a dwarf with the limbs of a child, the body of a man, and a finely developed intellectual head. He learned his letters and to read by calling the school children into the cabin as they passed, and also learned to write. He became a Baptist preacher, and after the war engaged in teaching colored children, and conducted the business correspondence of many of his colored neighbors. He is a man of blameless character, of unusual intelligence, speaks good English, and we put the story of his wrongs in his own language:

"On the night of the 5th of last May, after I had heard a great deal of what they had done in that neighborhood, they [the Ku Klux Klan] came. It was between 12 and 1 o'clock at night when I was awakened and heard the dogs barking, and something walking, very much like horses.... At last they came to my brother's door, which is in the same yard, and broke open the door and attacked his wife, and I heard her screaming and mourning.... At last I heard them have her in the yard. She was crying and the Ku-

Source: *Report of the Joint Select Committee to Inquire into the Condition of Affairs in the Late Insurrectionary States* (Washington, 1872).

Klux were whipping her to make her tell where I lived.... Some one then hit my door. It flew open. One ran in the house, and stopping about the middle of the house, which is a small cabin, he turned around, as it seemed to me as I lay there awake, and said, 'Who's here?' Then I knew they would take me, and I answered, 'I am here.' He shouted for joy, as it seemed, 'Here he is! Here he is! We have found him!' and he threw the bedclothes off of me and caught me by one arm, while another man took me by the other and they carried me into the yard between the houses.... The first thing they asked me was, 'Who did the burning? Who burned our houses?'—gin-houses, dwelling-houses and such. Some had been burned in the neighborhood. I told them it was not me; I could not burn houses; it was unreasonable to ask me. Then they hit me with their fists, and said I did it, I ordered it. They went on asking me didn't I tell the black men to ravish all the white women. No, I answered them. They struck me again with their fists on my breast, and then they went on....

They pointed pistols at me all around my head once or twice, as if they were going to shoot me, telling me they were going to kill me; wasn't I ready to die, and willing to die? Didn't I preach? That they came to kill me—all the time pointing pistols at me.... One said 'G-d d—n it, hush!' He had a horsewhip, and he told me to pull up my shirt, and he hit me. He told me at every lick, 'Hold up your shirt.' I made a moan every time he cut with the horsewhip. I reckon he struck me eight cuts right on the hip bone; it was almost the only place he could hit my body, my legs are so short—all my limbs drawn up and withered away with pain.... They all had disguises on. I then thought they would not kill me. One of them then took a strap, and buckled it around my neck and said, 'Let's take him to the river and drown him....'

They said 'Look here! Will you put a card in the paper next week like June Moore and Sol Hill?' They had been prevailed on to put a card in the paper to renounce all republicanism and never vote. I said, 'If I had the money to pay the expense, I could.' They said I could borrow, and gave me another lick. They asked me, 'Will you quit preaching?' I told them I did not know. I said that to save my life. They said I must stop the republican paper that was coming to Clay Hill. It has been only a few weeks since it stopped. The republican paper was then coming to me from Charleston. It came to my name. They said I must stop it, quit preaching, and put a card in the newspaper renouncing republicanism, and they would not kill me; but if I did not they would come back the next week and kill me."

45
Henry Blake

"AFTER FREEDOM, WE WORKED ON SHARES"

Henry Blake was born into slavery in Little Rock, Arkansas, and was approximately 80 years old when he was interviewed by the Works Progress Administration.

After freedom, we worked on shares a while. Then, we rented. When we worked on shares, we couldn't make nothing—just overalls, and something to eat. Half went to the white man, and you would destroy your half, if you weren't careful. A man that didn't know how to count would always lose. He might lose anyhow. The white folks didn't give no itemized statements. No, you just had to owe so much. No matter how good account you kept, you had to go by their account, and—now, brother, I'm telling you the truth about this—it's been that way for a long time. You had to take the white man's words and notes on everything. Anything you wanted you could get, if you were a good hand. If you didn't make no money, that's all right; they would advance you more. But you better not try to leave and get caught. They'd keep you in debt. They were sharp. Christmas come, you could take up twenty dollars in somethin'-to-eat and much as you wanted in whiskey. You could buy a gallon of whiskey—anything that kept you a slave. Because he was always right and you were always wrong, if there was a difference. If there was an argument, he would get mad and there would be a shooting take place.

Source: George P. Rawick, *The American Slave: A Composite Autobiography* (Westport, Conn., 1972) Ark. Narr., Vol. 8, 175-179.

46
Frederick Douglass

"THE SERFS OF RUSSIA ... WERE GIVEN THREE ACRES OF LAND"

Frederick Douglass assesses the meaning of emancipation in 1880.

How stands the case with the recently emancipated millions of colored people in our own country? What is their condition to-day? What is their relation to the people who formerly held them as slaves? These are important questions, and they are such as trouble the minds of thoughtful men of all colors, at home and abroad. By law, by the constitution of the United States, slavery has no existence in our country. The legal form has been abolished. By the law and the constitution, the Negro is a man and a citizen, and has all the rights and liberties guaranteed to any other variety of the human family, residing in the United States....

In pursuance of this idea, the Negro was made free, made a citizen, made eligible to hold office, to be a juryman, a legislator, and a magistrate. To this end, several amendments to the constitution were proposed, recommended, and adopted.... This is our condition on paper and parchment. If only from the national statute book we were left to learn the true condition of the colored race, the result would be altogether creditable to the American people....

We have laid the heavy hand of the constitution upon the matchless meanness of caste, as well as upon the hell-black crime of slavery.... But to-day, in most of the Southern States, the fourteenth and fifteenth amendments are virtually nullified.

The rights which they were intended to guarantee are denied and held in contempt. The citizenship granted in the fourteenth amendment is practically a mockery, and the right to vote, pro-

Source: *Life and Times of Frederick Douglass* (Boston, 1892).

vided for in the fifteenth amendment, is literally stamped out in face of government. The old master class is to-day triumphant, and the newly-enfranchised class in a condition but little above that in which they were found before the rebellion.

Do you ask me how, after all that has been done, this state of things has been made possible? I will tell you. Our reconstruction measures were radically defective. They left the former slave completely in the power of the old master, the loyal citizen in the hands of the disloyal rebel against the government. Wise, grand, and comprehensive in scope and desire as were the reconstruction measures, high and honorable as were the intentions of the statesmen by whom they were framed and adopted, time and experience, which try all things, have demonstrated that they did not successfully meet the case.

In the hurry and confusion of the hour, and the eager desire to have the Union restored, there was more care for the sublime superstructure of the republic than for the solid foundation upon which it could alone be upheld.... The old master class was not deprived of the power of life and death, which was the soul of the relation of master and slave. They could not, of course, sell their former slaves, but they retained the power to starve them to death, and wherever this power is held there is the power of slavery. He who can say to his fellow-man, "You shall serve me or starve," is a master and his subject is a slave.... Though no longer a slave, he is in a thralldom grievous and intolerable, compelled to work for whatever his employer is pleased to pay him, swindled out of his hard earnings by money orders redeemed in stores, compelled to pay the price of an acre of ground for its use during a single year, to pay four times more than a fair price for a pound of bacon and to be kept upon the narrowest margin between life and starvation....

When the serfs of Russia were emancipated, they were given three acres of ground upon which they could live and make a living. But not so when our slaves were emancipated. They were sent away empty-handed, without money, without friends and without a foot of land upon which to stand....

Greatness does not come on flowery beds of ease to any people. We must fight to win the prize. No people to whom liberty is given, can hold it as firmly and wear it as grandly as those who wrench liberty from the iron hand of the tyrant. The hardships and dangers involved in the struggle give strength and toughness to the character, and enable it to stand firm in storm as well as in sunshine.

BIBLIOGRAPHY

Although slavery is now one of the most intensively-studied topics in United States history, there was a long period during which it was largely ignored. The Progressive school of interpretation, which dominated the American history profession during the first half of the twentieth century, considered slavery to be less important than conflicts between classes, sections, and industrial and agrarian interests. Except for the works of a handful of African-American historians like Carter Woodson, Benjamin Quarles, and W.E.B. DuBois and Southern historians like Ulrich B. Phillips, slavery was regarded as an extraneous aspect of American history.

This prolonged period of scholarly neglect came to an end in the mid-1950s. Since the publication of Kenneth Stampp's *The Peculiar Institution* in 1956, no topic has produced a greater outpouring of important scholarly works or provoked more controversy than the study of slavery. In part, the explosion of scholarly interest in slavery reflected the increasing public concern with civil rights and race relations. It also reflected a recognition that slavery played a critical role in the settlement and economic development of the New World and the major political conflicts and alignments of the pre-Civil War period.

The study of slavery has contributed to a radical reshaping of the discipline of history, leading scholars to tap new sources of data and to employ new methods of analysis. Historical demographers have drawn upon census records to reconstruct slave birth and mortality rates and family and kinship patterns. Historical archeologists have studied slave quarters in order to reconstruct patterns of everyday life. Medical historians have scrutinized records of height, weight, and disease. Cultural historians have analyzed African-American folklore and religious beliefs and customs. The result has been to reconstruct life under slavery in all of its complexity. Recent scholarship has decisively demonstrated that slaves were active agents who succeeded in creating a rich and vital culture.

The modern boom in slavery studies began with Kenneth Stampp's *The Peculiar Institution* (1956). Contradicting the conclusions of a much earlier authority on slavery, Ulrich B. Phillips, Stampp argued that nineteenth-century slavery was a profitable institution; that slaves suffered severely from disease and physical maltreatment; that they were inadequately fed, clothed, and housed; and that they expressed their discontent by breaking tools and running away, as well as through more violent forms of resistance.

Stanley Elkins's *Slavery: A Problem in American Institutional Life* (1959), which came out three years after *The Peculiar Institution*, defined the issues that dominated subsequent scholarship. Drawing upon the work of two prominent Latin American historians, Gilberto Freyre and Frank Tannenbaum, Elkins argued that American slavery was much harsher and more exploitative than Latin American slavery. Indeed, Elkins likened Southern slave plantations to Nazi concentration camps, and argued that slavery was so brutal and inhumane that it stripped slaves of their African heritage and transformed them into docile, submissive figures.

Much subsequent scholarship on American slavery can be viewed as a rebuttal of Elkins's arguments. Instead of portraying slaves as passive objects of oppression, later scholars focused their attention on the intricate ways that slaves resisted and accommodated to slavery; the nature of the culture and community that African-Americans created within bondage; and the similarities and differences between Southern slavery and bondage elsewhere. If any single theme can be said to unify the remarkable outpouring of scholarship on slavery, it is African-Americans' extraordinary success in creating and sustaining vital kinship and cultural and religious traditions under conditions of extreme oppression. Among the important general studies that have emphasized slaves' capacity to resist slavery and establish separate communities are John B. Boles, *Black Southerners* (1983); John D. Blassingame, *The Slave Community* (1979); Eugene D. Genovese, *Roll, Jordan, Roll* (1974); Charles Joyner, *Down by the Riverside* (1984); Peter Kolchin, *American Slavery* (1993); and Leslie Howard Owens, *This Species of Property* (1976).

The modern study of slave culture traces its roots back to Melville J. Herskovit's *Myth of the Negro Past* (1941), which argued that many aspects of African-American culture—including art, family, folklore, language, and music—represented cultural survivals from West Africa. More recent studies have substituted the notion of syncretism—that is, a blending of African and European cultures—for Herskovit's concept of cultural survival. Valuable studies of slaves' culture and worldviews include Daniel J. Crowley, ed., *African Folklore in the New World* (1977); Dena J. Epstein, *Sinful Tunes and Spirituals* (1977); Joseph E. Holloway, *Africanisms in American Culture* (1990); Lawrence Levine, *Black Culture and Black Consciousness* (1977); Albert J. Raboteau, *Slave Religion* (1978); Mechal Sobel, *Travelin' On: The Slave Journey to an Afro-Baptist Faith* (1979); Sterling Stuckey, *Slave Culture* (1987); Michael Vlach, *The Afro-American Tradition in Decorative Arts* (1978); and Thomas L. Webber, *Deep Like the Rivers: Education in the Slave Quarter Community* (1978).

Since Elkins's study appeared, a number of historians have penetrated America's national boundaries to compare Southern slavery with other systems of slavery and forced labor. Important works that locate Southern slavery in a comparative perspective include Carl N. Degler, *Neither Black Nor White: Slavery and Race Relations in Brazil and the United States* (1971); Richard S. Dunn, *Sugar and Slaves* (1972); Herbert S. Klein, *Slavery in the Americas* (1967); and Peter Kolchin, *Unfree Labor: American Slavery and Russian Serfdom* (1987).

Not all of the scholars who have studied slavery are historians. Many economists, who are interested in the impact of slavery on economic growth, also conducted intensive research on the institution. The modern debate over the profitability of slavery and its impact on the Southern economy began with an article by Alfred H. Conrad and John R. Meyer entitled "The Economics of Slavery in the Antebellum South," which appeared in the *Journal of Political Economy* in 1958. Among the scholars inspired by Conrad and Meyer's approach were Robert William Fogel and Stanley L. Engerman, who used sophisticated econometric and statistical techniques in their highly controversial reinterpretation of the slave economy, *Time on the Cross* (1974). Relying on a wide array of quantitative data, this book argued that slavery was a highly profitable institution; that slave labor was highly efficient; that masters promoted stable nuclear families; and that slaves were healthy, well fed, rarely whipped, and seldom sold away from spouses. The volume produced withering criticisms that challenged the book's evidence, methods, and interpretations, including Herbert G. Gutman, *Slavery and the Numbers Game* (1975) and Paul A. David et al., *Reckoning with Slavery* (1976). Fogel responded to his critics' charges in 1989 with a volume entitled *Without Consent or Contract*, which synthesizes much recent quantitative research on slavery.

Until remarkably recently, there was a tendency to treat slavery as a static, unchanging institution. A number of recent volumes have begun to chronicle the historical evolution of American slavery. Valuable studies of colonial slavery include Timothy H. Breen and Stephen Innes, *"Myne Owne Ground": Race and Freedom on Virginia's Eastern Shore* (1980); Jay Coughtry, *The Notorious Triangle: Rhode Island and the Atlantic Slave Trade* (1981); Winthrop D. Jordan, *White Over Black* (1968); Herbert S. Klein, *Slavery in the Americas: Virginia and Cuba* (1967); Allan Kulikoff, *Tobacco and Slaves: Southern Culture in the Chesapeake* (1986); Daniel C. Littlefield, *Rice and Slaves: Ethnicity and the Slave Trade in Colonial South Carolina* (1981); Edgar J. McManus, *Black Bondage in the North* (1973); Edmund S. Morgan, *American Slavery, American Freedom* (1975); Gerald W. Mullin, *Flight and Rebellion: Slave Resistance in Virginia* (1972); Mechal Sobel, *The World They Made Together: Black and White Values in Eighteenth-Century Virginia* (1987); Thad W. Tate, *The Negro in Eighteenth-Century Williamsburg* (1966); Betty Wood, *Slavery in Colonial Georgia* (1984); Peter H. Wood, *Black Majority: Negroes in Colonial South Carolina* (1974); and Donald R. Wright, *African Americans in the Colonial Era* (1990).

For slavery during the revolutionary era, see Ira Berlin and Ronald Hoffman, eds., *Slavery and Freedom in the Age of the American Revolution* (1983); Sylvia R. Frey, *Water from the Rock: Black Resistance in a Revolutionary Age* (1991); Sidney and Emma N. Kaplan, *Black Presence in the Era of the American Revolution* (1989); Robert McColley, *Slavery and Jeffersonian Virginia* (1964); Duncan J. MacLeod, *Slavery, Race and the American Revolution* (1974); Donald L. Robinson, *Slavery in the Structure of American Politics* (1971); Shane White, *Somewhat More Independent: The End of Slavery in New York City* (1991); Arthur Zilversmit, *The First Emancipation: The Abolition of Slavery in the North* (1967).

No aspect of slavery has gone unexamined. The most profound analyses of the intellectual history of slavery are David Brion Davis, *The Problem of Slavery in Western Culture* (1967), *The Problem of Slavery in the Age of Revolution* (1975), and *Slavery and Human Progress* (1984); George M. Fredrickson, *The Black Image in the White Mind* (1971); Winthrop D. Jordan, *White Over Black: American Attitudes Toward the Negro* (1968); and Orlando Patterson, *Slavery and Social Death* (1982).

On the African slave trade, see Philip D. Curtin, *Africa Remembered: Narratives by West Africans* (1967), *The Atlantic Slave Trade* (1969), and *The Rise and Fall of the Plantation Complex* (1990); Basil Davidson, *Black Mother: Africa and the Atlantic Slave Trade* (1980); Herbert S. Klein, *The Middle Passage* (1978); Daniel P. Mannix, *Black Cargoes* (1962); Richard Olaniyan, ed., *African History and Culture* (1982); Oliver Ransford, *The Slave Trade* (1972); and James Rawley, *The Transatlantic Slave Trade* (1981).

On the historiography of slavery, see Charles B. Dew, "The Slavery Experience," in John B. Boles and Evely Thomas Nolen, eds., *Interpreting Southern History* (1987) and Peter J. Parish, *Slavery: History and Historians* (1989). The law of slavery is analyzed in A. Leon Higginbotham, Jr., *In the Matter of Color* (1978); Mark Tushnet, *The American Law of Slavery* (1981); and Alan Watson, *Slave Law in the Americas* (1989). On slave management, see James O. Breeden, ed., *Advice Among Masters* (1980); William K. Scarborough, *The Overseer* (1966); and William L. Van Deburg, *The Slave Drivers* (1979).

Women's lives under slavery are skillfully explored in Elizabeth Fox-Genovese, *Within the Plantation Household: Black and White Women of the Old South* (1988); Jacqueline Jones, *Labor of Love, Labor of Sorrow* (1985); and Deborah Gray White, *Ar'n't I a Woman* (1985). On the slave family, see Herbert G. Gutman, *The Black Family in Slavery and Freedom* (1976) and Cheryll Ann Cody, "There Was No 'Absalom' on the Ball Plantations: Slave Naming Practices in the South Carolina Low Country," *American Historical Review* (1988). Medical histories of slavery include Kenneth F. Kiple and Virginia Himmelsteib King, *Another Dimension to the Black Diaspora: Diet, Disease, and Racism* (1981) and Todd L. Savitt, *Medicine and Slavery* (1978). For urban slavery, see Claudia D. Goldin, *Urban Slavery in the American South* (1976) and Richard C. Wade, *Slavery in the Cities* (1964). On free blacks, see Ira Berlin, *Slaves Without Masters: The Free Negro in the Antebellum South* (1974); Leonard P. Curry, *The Free Black in Urban America* (1981); and Michael P. Johnson and James L. Roark, *Black Masters* (1984) and *No Chariot Let Down: Charleston's Free People of Color* (1984). On slave narratives, see Charles T. Davis and Henry Louis Gates, Jr., *The Slaves Narrative* (1985) and Marion Wilson Starling, *The Slave Narrative* (1981). For Frederick Douglass, see William S. McFeely, *Frederick Douglass* (1991); Waldo E. Martin Jr., *The Mind of Frederick Douglass* (1985); and Dickson J. Preston, *Young Frederick Douglass* (1985).

Specialized studies that are especially worthy of note are

Michael Craton, ed., *Roots and Branches: Current Directions in Slave Studies* (1979); Barbara Jean Fields, *Slavery and Freedom on the Middle Ground: Maryland* (1985); Eugene D. Genovese, *From Rebellion to Revolution: Afro-American Slave Revolts* (1979); Janet Sharp Hermann, *Pursuit of a Dream* (1981); Ronald L. Lewis, *Coal, Iron, and Slaves* (1979); Melton A. McLaurin, *Celia: A Slave* (1991); Stephen B. Oates, *The Fires of Jubilee: Nat Turner's Fierce Rebellion* (1975); Willie Lee Rose, ed., *A Documentary History of Slavery in North America* (1976); Robert S. Starobin, *Industrial Slavery in the Old South* (1970).

A large number of important recent studies have explored slavery's aftermath. Among these important recent works that focus on the black experience during the Civil War and Reconstruction are Eric Foner, *Nothing But Freedom* (1983) and *Reconstruction* (1988); Joseph T. Glatthaar, *Forged in Battle: The Civil War Alliance Between Black Soldiers and White Officers* (1990); Thomas Holt, *Black Over White* (1977); Peter Kolchin, *First Freedom* (1972); Leon Litwack, *"Been in the Storm So Long"* (1979); Jay R. Mandle, *Not Slave, Not Free* (1992); Clarence L. Mohr, *On the Threshold of Freedom: Masters and Slaves in Civil War Georgia* (1986); George C. Rable, *But There Was No Peace* (1984); Roger L. Ransom and Richard Sutch, *One Kind of Freedom* (1977); Willie Lee Rose, *Rehearsal for Reconstruction* (1964); Joel Williamson, *After Slavery* (1965) and *A Rage for Order* (1986).